LOVE YOUR HOME

Secrets to a Successful Space

DERMOT BANNON

GILL & MACMILLAN

Dedication

For my dad, Jim

Gill & Macmillan
Hume Avenue, Park West, Dublin 12
www.gillmacmillanbooks.ie

© Dermot Bannon 2014
978 07171 6448 6

Edited by Emma Cullinan
Design by www.grahamthew.com
Print origination by Design Image
Printed by Printer Trento Srl, Italy

This book is typeset in 11 pt Arquitecta Book on 15 pt leading

The paper used in this book comes from the wood pulp of managed forests. For every tree felled, at least one tree is planted, thereby renewing natural resources.

A CIP catalogue record for this book is available from the British Library.

5 4 3

CONTENTS

The Author

Dermot Bannon is a leading voice in modern Irish architectural design. He has hosted RTÉ's *Room to Improve* TV series since 2007, transforming the homes and lives of hundreds of clients. He set up his own practice, Dermot Bannon Architects (DBA), in 2008. He lives in Drumcondra with his wife and three children.

Acknowledgements

A huge amount of work goes into publishing a book, and just as no architect can build a house alone, no author could complete the task without the assistance of many people behind the scenes.

I must start by thanking my creative and gifted editor, Emma Cullinan, to whom I owe a huge debt of gratitude. Emma took my ideas and our ramblings on architecture and made them into a cohesive text – this wouldn't be the book it is without her.

Thank you to all the dedicated, hard-working and infinitely patient staff at Gill & Macmillan for pulling it all together. Special mention must go to Deirdre Nolan, Deirdre Rennison Kunz, Jen Patton and Teresa Daly, and to Kristin Jensen, the external copy-editor.

Thank you to all at Coco TV for believing in me and giving me my big break, particularly Linda Cullen, Hilary O'Donovan, Jane Wardrop, Stuart Switzer, Luke McManus, Stevie Vickers, Joanne McGrath and Patricia Power. Working on and filming *Room to Improve* for the last number of years has been an incredible experience with a wonderful team that I am very proud to be part of.

Thank you also to the team at RTÉ, especially Grainne McAleer for her constant support.

Thank you to all at the RIAI for their encouragement, and thanks to Kathryn Meghen for her help and guidance in this book.

A big thank you to all the really talented team at Dermot Bannon Architects, especially Ian Hurley, Ger Cleary, Donal Farrelly, Sean Fogarty, Donnachadh O'Sullivan, Peter McEleney and Lorna Sweeney.

Thanks to my mum, Mary, my brother, Padraig, and my sister, Fionnuala, for being there always.

And finally, thanks to my wonderful wife, Louise, and my amazing children, Sarah, James and Tom, who inspire me every day and have taught me that the most important thing about my home is them!

Dermot

Introduction:

My Passion
for Design

FIRST LOVE

My love of architecture is grounded in regionalism (regionalism is where a building is influenced by and deeply rooted in its region or place) and it always has been. When people would say 'That's a really cool building', I never got that. For me, architecture was never about the building, the single entity. What floated my boat was places, streets, villages. Buildings are shaped by landscapes, going from fields to streetscapes, to steps up to a building, to the railings and thresholds.

I grew up in Malahide, north of Dublin. It was a small village centred around a diamond, with a mix of Georgian and Victorian buildings (notably on Church Road) and urban sprawl. It used to be a crossroads and an old fishing village with a boatyard where my friends and I would steal away for a crafty cigarette. That all died away and it became a suburb of Dublin. Since it is on

Collins Agency

a train line, Malahide became a commuter town and started to grow in the 1970s and 1980s. I loved seeing how it became in-filled, turning into a complete village.

My dad was at the forefront of this as the chair of the Malahide Community Council. Malahide commissioned a development control plan from

Dermot Bannon Architects

architect Patrick Shaffrey. I saw the draft proposals lying around the house when I was young, and even read them.

Dad, a horticulturalist, was also involved in Tidy Towns and I was too, spending summers watering other people's window boxes and tidying buildings.

We eventually won the Tidy Towns award, which we felt was a huge achievement for a suburb, as the competition was always won by small villages and we were dealing with a town that was bigger than Kilkenny.

When I was seven I went from suburban Ireland to Cairo in Egypt, a dusty city full of hustle and bustle, with trams and people living on the street, between stalls – streets were hugely important places. There was a massive architectural heritage and some buildings were being rebuilt, as Israel and Egypt were at war at the time over the Sinai Desert. As a family we spent a lot of time in the UN facility; the Irish army was in Egypt on a peace-keeping mission.

Cairo was such a contrast to Malahide. Everyone lived in apartments. There was no such thing as a house on its own; there was always somebody above or below you. We were on the 11th floor. I had never been up so high, looking out over the city and across to the Nile.

I became obsessed with geography, countries and cities. I was fascinated by atlases and traced parts of one every night for a year. I would bring an atlas to the swimming pool and draw countries during the break. I remember sitting and looking at America for hours, studying the roads and mountains. I revisited this recently with Google Maps, looking into the depths of Alaska late at night. It has come full circle.

My appreciation of the Irish countryside and farm buildings came from my parents. Mum is from Wexford and Dad was from Waterford and we spent our summers there. With rural structures, it was not about the buildings themselves but how they were knit into the landscape – the way in which a vernacular farmhouse is perpendicular to the road, how the house is connected to the cow house, and the cow house is connected to the barn and so on. The buildings snake around into the landscape and create courtyards, in-between places like a piazza in Perugia, but here on a very small scale.

When you drive into towns (such as Birr) and even small villages in Ireland, I love the way it suddenly becomes urban, with quite grand places. Groups of buildings can create impressive spaces, like those on Merrion and Fitzwilliam squares in Dublin. I still get a kick out of walking around St Stephen's Green. It is the same in London. On their own the houses are nothing special, but collectively they are incredible.

FAMILY TRAITS

I am the first architect in our family but there is creativity there, especially on my mother's side. She taught home economics, she made all of our clothes and she loved to write letters. And I loved getting them from her in college; they were beautifully written. Mum used to make extravagant cakes with complicated structures at Christmas to raffle for charity and I'd be heavily involved in that. If she needed a structure, such as an arch, or figures for a crib, I made them.

Dermot Bannon Architects/Enda Cavanagh

Dad didn't consider himself creative, but he was. As a horticulturalist he developed his own breed of roses, amongst other things. His passion for landscape and planting rubbed off on me. Whatever he was doing, he would ask, 'How does it interact with the landscape?' He taught me about indigenous planting. He hated television programmes that finished a garden in one day. For Dad, you planted things and really didn't see a complete garden for many years. What my parents did in their everyday lives was creative without them realising it.

I can't recall wanting to do anything else but architecture from the age of eight. I was always building. Lego was the first thing I ever played with. I was far more into that than sports – when I was playing football I would be dreaming of getting back to Lego. I'd have it all covered in a blanket so no one would take it away. I didn't give it up until I was 12 or 13, which was probably way too old, but it was my guilty pleasure.

But I didn't stay at that scale. When my aunt and uncle built an extension, there was a big stack of bricks on site that my cousin and I would play with. Building with real bricks was the coolest thing. I always loved making things.

Another aunt renovated a really old Georgian house in Waterford and I loved to see how it was progressing. She was an artist and got me into drawing, painting and sketching, which, surprisingly, was something I did in my first year at Hull University.

LESSONS IN CREATIVITY

I studied architecture in Hull. My parents were really nervous about me heading overseas at the age of 17, but it didn't faze me. This was my dream – I wasn't going to take another course – so if it meant I had to go to the UK, then I was going.

The first year was tough. I thought we would be designing buildings, but instead they set us loose on sculptures, poems, paintings and making music – one project was about *Lord of the Flies* – to see how we felt about it and to get us to express ourselves. It was disassembling before assembling through architecture in order to see things differently, to release the magic, to see the

shadow and the light. 'What the hell has this got to do with architecture?' I thought. But then I enjoyed it, even though it came slowly. After that I settled into college and loved it.

The architecture school at Hull was very much about making places, and not about ego buildings. In a lot of our projects we would take a whole chunk of city and redesign that first in order to understand how that worked before putting a building into it. How could you put a building in there before you understood how the streetscape worked?

IRELAND'S CALL

I came back to Ireland at the start of the boom in 1997. I had left during a recession and my parents honestly thought I would never return. One of the great things about the boom was that I could decide what projects I wanted to do. I worked on schools and hospitals and learned about creating spaces that were nurturing for people.

Everything was so prescribed in school classrooms that I made sure I was creative in the communal spaces, scraping 5mm here and there to help social interaction. In one of the first buildings I worked on I made a corridor narrow at one end and wider at the other so that instead of being a corridor all the way, there was a social space, almost another room, at one end.

In starting to examine how people use buildings, there was a natural progression on to homes. I always had a passion for houses and the work of Corbusier, Carlo Scarpa, Alvar Aalto, Mies van der Rohe, Charles Rennie Mackintosh – all the heroes.

Dermot Bannon Architects/Ros Kavanagh

Today I am constantly inspired by other Irish architects, my contemporaries whose skill and vision result in beautiful, authentic buildings created with verve and integrity. I have gratefully used their work throughout this book to demonstrate how great design can transform a living space.

SCREEN BREAK

I began on television with *House Hunters*. I got the job through an ad on the Royal Institute of the Architects of Ireland website. The programme guided people around older houses so that they didn't ignore doer-uppers when they were looking for a place to buy.

At the time, stamp duty was huge. I would say to people, 'Instead of paying €90,000 in tax on a new home, why don't you fix what's wrong with your existing home?' Coco TV went to RTÉ with that idea and I got the job presenting *Room to Improve* in 2007 (I set up my own practice a year later). It is a niche I've fallen into and I love it.

Some people who watch the programme say, 'You must have a lot of patience in dealing with reluctant clients.' But I don't see it like that. The type of houses and architecture we have has gone largely unchallenged in this country for so long that I do come up against resistance when it goes a bit beyond people's comfort zone. But I always feel that somebody needs to love the building. It can't be all about people – if you concentrate on the building and the design, then everything else will fall into place.

My two favourite architects are Carlo Scarpa and Luigi Snozzi, who were very much about creating places rather than an individual building.

My big love affair in college was Snozzi. He designed a whole town in Switzerland called Monte Carrasso. When asked to design a building, he said, 'Guys, your town is fractured.' He would then draw a city and show how his building fitted into it.

PHOTO CREDITS

Thank you to all of the architects and photographers whose work has graced these pages and made this publication possible. They have all been generous and inspiring, and their work is a testament to Irish architectural talent. Thank you also to the Royal Institute of the Architects of Ireland (RIAI) for their support and assistance in sourcing images.

ARCHITECTS

A2 Architects
Photos: 101TL, 189
www.a2.ie
3 Great Strand Street, Dublin 1
+353 (0)1 872 7393
office@a2.ie

Ailtir(eacht)
Photos: 48B, 50, 123, 128–9, 144, 155B, 161L, 162B, 163C, 177, 186B
www.ailtir.net
37 North Great Georges Street, Dublin 1
+353 (0)1 878 0050
info@ailtir.net

Amanda Bone Architects
Photos © Ros Kavanagh: 16, 21T, 23, 43T, 63T, 91T, 107TR, 122T, 140B, 150B, 169B
www.amandabonearchitects.ie
1 Upper Kilmacud Road, Dundrum, Dublin 14
+353 (0)1 298 9197

Aughey O'Flaherty Architects
Photos © Grand Designs: 74T, 135B
Photos © Marie-Louise Halpenny: 35, 42T, 52T, 57, 75T, 90B, 91B, 108, 115T, 124, 132B, 134B, 139T, 174BL, 174BR, 183B
Photos © Paul Tierney: 69T, 73B, 167, 195
www.aof.ie
32 Nassau Street, Dublin 2
+353 (0)1 672 9932
hello@aof.ie

box architecture
Photos © Paul Tierney: 17, 41, 53T, 84B, 87B, 88B, 90T, 98–9
Photos © Hugh Glynn: 150T, 174T
www.box.ie
30 Blackpitts, Dublin 8
+353 (0)1 473 7106
info@box.ie

Dermot Bannon Architects
Photos © Dermot Bannon: 2B, 4–5, 8B, 11, 19TR, 26, 32B, 38R, 43B, 45B, 47, 49, 53B, 60, 71T, 72T, 75B, 78T, 86T, 95R, 101TR, 111C, 111B, 113C, 119TL, 130T, 134T, 136T, 138, 140T, 167R, 169T, 196, 197, 198, 198, 200, 201
Photos © Enda Cavanagh: 6–7, 8T, 14–15, 29, 36–7, 44B, 51B, 59, 105T, 114, 119B, 127, 139B, 146T, 147, 151, 159T, 160T, 163B, 164T, 165, 181, 190–91, 193T
Photos © Ros Kavanagh: vi–1, 10, 42B, 48TR, 88T, 100B, 112TR, 113T, 121T, 121B, 135T, 175BL
www.dermotbannonarchitects.com
The Malthouse, Distillery Court,
537 North Circular Road, Dublin 1
+353 (0)1 855 0172 / +353 (0)86 022 2026
info@dermotbannonarchitects.com

DMVF
Photos © Ros Kavanagh: 20, 66T, 79T, 93T, 93B, 112TL, 149, 154B, 157T
www.dmvf.ie
278 Lower Rathmines Road, Dublin 6 / 87 Main Street, Bray, Co. Wicklow
+353 (0)1 407 1080
info@dmvf.ie

Donaghy & Dimond Architects
Photos © Donaghy & Dimond Architects: 45T, 76B, 110B, 112B, 132T, 145B
Photos © Dennis Gilbert: 77L, 152
Photos © Marie-Louise Halpenny: 66B, 83T, 87TR, 162T
Photos © Ros Kavanagh: 24BR, 58T, 62B, 64T, 86B, 92, 100T, 115B, 120, 133T
Photos © Philip Lauterbach: 73T, 105B, 143, 153
Photos © Luke White: 104T, 146BR, 156T, 158BL, 162C
www.donaghydimond.ie
41 Francis Street, Dublin 8
+353 (0)1 416 8132
info@donaghydimond.ie

Donal Colfer
Photos © Alice Clancy: 30–31L, 58B, 95L, 96, 104B, 117, 136B, 157B, 159B
www.donalcolfer.ie
Slade, Hook Head, New Ross, Co. Wexford
+353 (0)86 318 8671
info@donalcolfer.ie

FKL Architects
Photos © FKL Architects: 141T
Photos © Verena Hilgenfeld: 38L, 106, 131B, 164B, 168B
Photos © Ros Kavanagh: 67, 89
Photos © Paul Tierney: 80–81
www.fklarchitects.com
4 Stable Lane, Cambridge Road, Rathmines, Dublin 6
+353 (0)1 473 6350
design@fklarchitects.com

Garbhan Doran Architects
Photos: 39, 40, 51T, 71B, 85BR, 109, 173, 182
www.garbhandoranarchitects.com
68 Dame Street, Dublin 2
+353 (0)1 670 6030 /
+353 (0)86 832 2161
mail@garbhandoranarchitects.com

GKMP Architects
Photos © Alice Clancy: 32T, 34, 54T, 62T, 88C, 137, 179, 188
Photos © Paul Tierney: 19B, 33, 97
www.gkmp.ie
19a Baggot Street Upper, Dublin 4
+353 (0)1 668 6120
info@gkmp.ie

John Feely Architects
Photos © Ros Kavanagh: 19TL, 56B, 130B, 168T, 175R, 176
www.johnfeely.ie
171 Botanic Road, Glasnevin, Dublin 9
+353 (0)1 857 0589
johnfeelyarchitects@eircom.net

Lawrence and Long Architects
Photos © Marie-Louise Halpenny: 22, 25, 54B, 56T, 113B, 126, 154T, 155T, 187
www.lawrenceandlong.com
43 Fitzwilliam Square, Dublin 2
+353 (0)1 661 9206
info@lawrenceandlong.com

Michael Kelly Architect
Photo © Gergely Lad: 65
www.michaelkellyarchitect.ie
45 Lower Baggot Street, Dublin 2
+353 (0)1 676 9780
mkellyarch@eircom.net

Peter Legge Associates
Photos: 24BL, 52B, 55, 61B, 63B, 68T, 69B, 74C, 75C, 79B, 94T, 116, 118T, 125, 133B, 141B, 142, 146BL, 156B, 158BR, 158T, 161R, 163T
Peter Legge Associates with John Monahan
Photos: 27, 110T, 148B, 172B
www.plaarchitects.ie
The Studio (green door), Abbey Court, Abbey Road, Blackrock, Co. Dublin
+353 (0)1 230 2851 /
+353 (0)1 230 2852
mail@plaarchitects.ie

PG Architects
Photos: 46, 48TL, 74B, 131T, 160B, 178, 185T, 192
www.pgarchitects.ie
'Woodfield House', Hill of Down, Enfield, Co. Meath
+353 (0)46 955 6991 /
+353 (0)87 239 2150
info@pgarchitects.ie

Robert Bourke Architects
Photos © Alice Clancy: 28, 64B, 82, 101B, 133C, 145T
www.rba.ie
37 North Great George's Street, Dublin 1
+353 (0)1 872 7904 /
+353 (0)85 148 8616
studio@rba.ie

Ryan Kennihan Architects
Photos © Alice Clancy: 72B, 77R, 83B, 85TL, 87TL, 166L, 194
www.rwka.com
30 Mountjoy Square, Dublin 1
+353 (0)1 888 1916
office@rwka.com

Sterrin O'Shea Architects
Photos: 18, 21B, 31TR, 44T, 61T, 70, 73C, 78B, 84T, 94B, 102–3, 107B, 111T, 119TR, 122B, 148T, 171B, 172T, 183T, 185B, 186T, 193B
www.sosa.ie
sterrinoshea@sosa.ie

Steve Larkin Architects
Photos © Alice Clancy: 68B, 76T, 107TL, 118B, 170, 180, 184
www.stevelarkinarchitects.ie
4 Castle Street, Dublin 2
+353 (0)1 478 9152 /
+353 (0)87 980 7590
stevelarkinarchitects@gmail.com

PHOTOGRAPHERS

Enda Cavanagh Photography
www.endacavanagh.com
111 Harbour View, Crofton Road, Dun Laoghaire, Co. Dublin
+353 (0)1 284 5430 /
+353 (0)87 650 1537
photos@endacavanagh.com

Alice Clancy
www.aliceclancy.com
+353 (0)86 343 9156
clancyalice@yahoo.co.uk

Peter Cook
www.petercookphoto.com

Dennis Gilbert
www.dennisgilbert.com

Hugh Glynn
13–14 Liberty Lane, Camden Row, Dublin 8
+353 (0)1 475 6038 /
+353 (0)86 333 9994
hugh.glynn@gmail.com

Marie-Louise Halpenny
www.marielouisehalpenny.com
Studio, 2 Rus In Urbe, Lower Glenageary Road, Dun Laoghaire, Co. Dublin
+353 (0)1 663 8565 /
+353 (0)87 667 6541
info@marielouisehalpenny.com

Verena Hilgenfeld
www.imagearchitecture.eu
+49 179 764 9436
info@imagearchitecture.eu

Ros Kavanagh
www.roskavanagh.com
+353 (0)86 220 7227
ros@roskavanagh.com

Philip Lauterbach
www.plpix.com
+353 (0)86 858 0933
production@plpix.com

Paul Tierney
www.paultierney.com
+353 (0)86 385 8800

Luke White
www.lukewhite.com
+ 44 (0)79 762 77410
info@lukewhite.com

PHOTO AGENCIES

Alamy: 3T, 3B, 9C, 9B
Collins Agency: 2T
Shutterstock: 9T

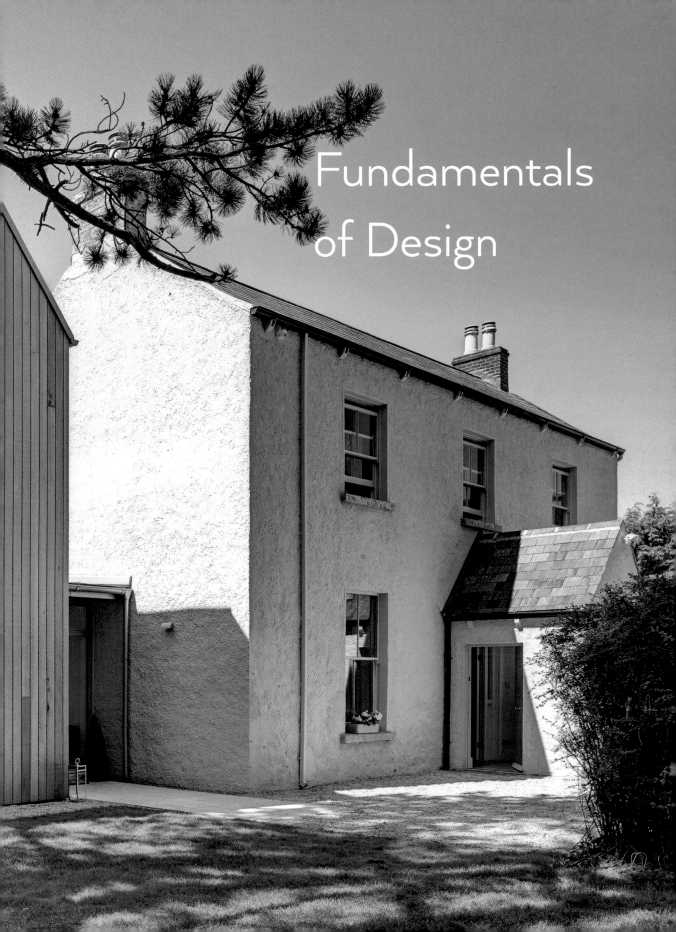

Fundamentals
of Design

CHAPTER 1

BRINGING THE OUTSIDE IN

CONNECTIONS

We all have a fundamental need to connect with nature. People are so rooted in the outdoors that rooms without a view feel like prisons to us. When we spend a lot of time in a space, we need to be able to refresh ourselves by looking out at a world that is different to the one we are in. And that is why homes must connect to, and have some sort of view of, the outdoors.

Architects will spend time on a site honing in on factors such as views and connections to outside spaces that can influence the design. Where someone else might just see a boring field, an architect could see a hill, a distant church spire or one simple tree.

When considering a home and its views, you create a fingerprint of the house, a design that can only work in that spot. For example, when I was designing my cousin's house we climbed up on the scaffolding to find that at a certain point, we could see a church spire. So we turned the stairs around, and now when people reach the landing, they can see that spire.

INSIDE OUT

We often think of buildings as entities that turn inwards, and yet it is so important to orientate them to the exterior. There are many ways of doing this, including the addition of balconies and terraces and well-designed glass openings.

Amanda Bone Architects/Ros Kavanagh

WINDOWS ON THE WORLD

One way to improve the link between the inside and outside is to increase the size of windows. If money is tight, then the best option is probably to lower them – standard windows are usually about 2 or 3 feet off the ground – because it doesn't involve complex structural work. You can take out the blockwork beneath a window knowing that it is supported from above. Making windows wider could involve more structural work, unless the structural lintel is wider than the existing window.

WONDER WALL

If you have a good outside space, there is nothing nicer than a large glazed wall. People still worry about privacy, but there are many ways around this, including having the glazing at the back of the house (assuming it works with the orientation). As a general rule, when connecting to the exterior in this way, the size of the glazing should be at least the equivalent of 25 per cent of the floor area in the room, and up to about 50 per cent. Sometimes a room is *too* open, which is why there is an upper limit to the size of glass. Having said that, if you are using the glazed wall in a room that you are connecting to another room that has little or no glass, then you can add its floor space into the calculation.

Sterrin O'Shea Architects

PICTURE THIS

This idea of having too much of a good thing (with copious amounts of glazing) extends to views, which can be spoiled with huge windows that gaze incessantly at them, turning the vista into wallpaper. Instead, control the view and capture it in glimpses. This way, you build up to the grand finale.

You can see how this was done in older houses (notwithstanding the fact that glass was also kept in check because it was expensive). For instance, Powerscourt, in County Wicklow, doesn't have large conservatories looking at the Sugarloaf; instead, you only get glimpses of the mountain in the transition spaces.

You can have the opening in a place that you walk through or in rooms you might relax in. Consider a window seat or bench (which is relatively cheap to do) at such a spot to draw you to the space and allow the connection to the outside. With these framed openings, you won't have the same view day in, day out. I often find that I'll walk a site with a farmer and my jaw drops at the stunning view, but when I mention it they say, 'Oh, yeah, I suppose so.' If you work in the shadow of an amazing view like a waterfall or mountain all day long, it almost disappears. But if you choose one room to capture the view in, then it remains special. It doesn't have to be a spectacular landmark – you might have a vista that includes something as simple as the sun hitting off a big tree.

John Feely Architects/Ros Kavanagh

Dermot Bannon Architects

GKMP Architects/Paul Tierney

BRINGING THE OUTSIDE IN   19

POSITIVE SPACES

Humans love to be enclosed, which is worth remembering when creating spaces outside. Even when making a porch or balcony, it feels better if it is slightly recessed into the building. Balconies or windowsills are important, not only to extend the feeling of the interior space, but to draw the eye outside. A balcony is more likely to be used if it is a good size (a minimum of 2 square metres) and has tables and chairs on it.

Having 'walls' around us creates a positive space. That is why we prefer Italian piazzas, courtyards, L-shaped buildings or small Georgian squares rather than vast expanses of leftover space, such as those which failed in apartment complexes, where we feel exposed. Having a 'room' in a garden bounded by hedges, fences or trellises helps with the transition from an inside room to an outside den, rather than stepping into a massive abyss. Its position should be planned carefully, perhaps capturing a sunny spot.

You can see this in places such as Russborough House, with its kitchen gardens and walled gardens. In Dublin's Phoenix Park, the walled garden at the visitors' centre is a lovely place to sit in. One of my clients in Wicklow has an amazing view of the Sugarloaf and I am creating an outside room, defined by trellises and pergolas, to frame the view because it is so big. It's an architectural idea that the clients have never seen before, so they don't want it – they think it is a waste of money – but I am pushing for it.

Amanda Bone Architects/Ros Kavanagh

Sterrin O'Shea Architects

In Ireland we like to be able to drive cars the whole way around a house, bringing them to the front or back door, which makes positive spaces difficult to achieve. You end up with a ring of tarmac outside the home and so you can't connect to the land or outdoor rooms.

OUT TO PLAY

Adults tend to use gardens to chill out and relax in, while children use them to create another world. When I was a kid we had a forklift pallet in our garden, which we made into so many things: a house, a boat, an airplane, a car. It also became a tunnel and a ramp for bikes. We had it for two years, until it finally broke.

Children will try to imagine all sorts of things. Shrubs and bushes become houses, plants are crushed with water to make 'perfume'. Gardens allow children that bit of freedom. It's their world, away from adults.

We have two massive trees at the end of our garden where I have put treehouses and swings. There is also a shed here. The children spend most of their time under those trees, which cast shadows so we don't even worry about them getting sunburnt. The tree canopy comes right down in summer – you have to duck your head under to get in – so in this spot they can be in another, private world.

Lawrence and Long Architects/Marie-Louise Halpenny

CHAPTER 2

LIGHT AND SPACE

NATURAL LIGHT

Light is what architecture is all about. It is as fundamental for the soul as air, fire, earth and water. Light has been one of the key elements of architecture since the Modern movement began (and glass technology improved) at the turn of the 20th century.

Yet light has traditionally been lacking in Irish homes. Many old cottages only have windows on the south side and none on the north. This is for two reasons. The first is that there used to be a tax on glass. People designed around this, which is why in old houses you often see lovely splayed window surrounds to maximise the light entering a home.

The other reason is that glass had poor thermal properties (windows let the cold in), so putting in large sheets of single-glazing made a house hard to heat. And all fuel had to be carried, be it coal, wood or peat. That is also why there were no windows on the north side – to bolster the home against wind and rain.

Peter Legge Associates

Donaghy & Dimond Architects/Ros Kavanagh

In the 1970s oil became cheaper and people began to introduce more natural light into homes. Now glass technology has improved and windows can be made with incredibly low U-values (meaning it doesn't let cold through), so you can now have large glazed areas without heat loss.

LIGHT MOTIVE

Human beings have phototrophic tendencies (phototrophs are organisms that create energy from light and it is seen in plants leaning towards the sun). We need light and instinctively search for it. People move to the part of a room where there is natural light and children instinctively play in pools of light.

Light can even motivate people. My happiest time as a student was working beside a window, with no computer (which often require blinds to be drawn). I always put my drawing board perpendicular to the window so that light came in on top of the board and I had a view out. Because it was the nicest place to be, instead of looking for something else to do, I would be pulled to the drawing board. If a chair or bed had been there, I would have sat on those. Because the board was in the nicest place, even if I had a cigarette (I've given up now) or was having a coffee break, I would sit there and doodle away subconsciously.

But we don't need to be bathed in natural light all the time. Variations are better, working with light and shadow, cold and warmth, as if the home were a painting. The spaces we move through, such as corridors, can have low levels of light, while the places in which people spend time have higher light levels. You can create low-light cosy nooks, have views out of a north-facing window and sit around evening fires that offer warmth in more than one way. Lighting candles also achieves this effect.

FOLLOW THE SUN

So how do you design or refurbish a home that brings outside light in? I am surprised by how many of my clients who have lived in a house for 10 or 20 years still don't know where the sun rises and sets or where south is. Some people have lost all the connection to light.

Peter Legge Associates with John Monahan

Start by finding out the orientation of your home, and therefore where the sun and light are, with a compass or smartphone. As we are all taught as children, the sun rises in the east and sets in the west, and good design will involve locating rooms in a home to follow that path, starting by putting bedrooms on the east side so that you wake to the rising sun.

I always ask my clients about their sequence of activities throughout their day. If you work at home you could put the study in the east, while the kitchen, for those who are in there a lot in the morning having breakfast or preparing food for later, should be on the south-east side of a home. The dining or living room can be in the west.

A CHANGE IN THINKING

Following the sun may mean defying tradition and having the kitchen at the front of the house and the living room at the back. We are still caught up with the idea that the living room must be to the front.

Some clients of mine have streams of natural light coming in through the front of their house, into a room they don't use during the day. They spend their time in the kitchen at the back, where there is little natural light, and in the evening they go to the front room, which has been filled with light all day, and close the curtains to watch the

telly. The house is a long, low bungalow in which there is huge potential to have a light-filled living space. I am trying to get them to flip the house, but they have a psychological barrier about that because they say there is no privacy at the front, even though it is 30 metres away from the road and it would be possible to plant hedges or make a screen. They want a solution other than moving the room.

This is not unusual. So many people in Irish bungalows have the living room to the front and the kitchen at the back, sitting in a half-light. To many, the effects of light are not quantifiable. People who enjoy a bright, sunny room imagine its ambiance is due to the décor – the furniture and paint colour. So people will see a beautiful south-facing room and ask about the paint colour, which they then use in their own north-facing room only to wonder why it doesn't work there.

GKMP Architects/Alice Clancy

THROUGH THE ROOF

If your house is in shadow because of nearby buildings or trees, a good way of increasing light levels is via the roof. A rooflight is a great way to bring light into the middle of a house, into internal rooms or into corridors that you have no chance of getting a window into. It can bring in sun all day long, as the roof surface is usually completely open to the sky all the time.

OPENING UP

The easiest way to bring in light is to have large south-facing windows. It is worth spending money on enlarging these, perhaps by taking a windowsill close to the ground (up to about 450mm). Or you can introduce a window seat. There is nothing nicer as the sunlight comes streaming in, creating a place to read or an extra space for children to play in.

You do need to be careful with large areas of glazing – it can overheat in the summer, although in winter the solar gain can reduce heating bills. A good trick is to put in an overhang to protect the interior from the midday sun. It can be at such

a height that in winter, when the sun is lower, the rays run beneath the overhang, warming the house. Architects can plan this accurately with specialist diagrams that map the sun's path and shadows at different times of the day and year.

Deciduous trees can also naturally work with large south-facing glass. Their leaves in summer create shade, and when the leaves fall in the autumn, leaving bare branches in winter, more sun will reach the glazing.

Clients who have been persuaded to have bright living spaces have literally seen the light and are delighted. They love being in a bright, airy space and realise it's something that works.

VOIDS, VOLUMES AND EXCITING SPACES

··

Where ceiling heights are concerned, we have entered a bit of a race to the bottom. The minimum height of 8 feet (or 2.4 metres) has now become a standard. You rarely find higher ceilings, which are seen as a luxury. We need to rethink this, especially when extending, when it's worth looking at connecting vertically rather than just thinking horizontally. Homes can be lovely when they have a sense of verticality.

The FKL Architects' A-House in Rathmines, Dublin, is a perfect example. A double-height void running up from the living, dining and kitchen area downstairs is at the back of the house, where a glazed wall looks onto the garden. This brings lots of natural light into the house, into both the downstairs area and upstairs, into the living room on one side of the first floor and into bedrooms on the other. It also creates a dramatic space and interesting vistas through the house, diagonally, across and up.

In a project of mine in Sutton, County Dublin, the back of the house is north-facing (like the Rathmines house) and we have put in a double-height tower at the back that connects the ground floor to an upstairs mezzanine, creating a majestic space at the back of the house that lets in loads of light. Sun also comes in through rooflights, so that parts of the house that have never been illuminated before are now flooded with light, both in the L-shaped kitchen and dining room on the ground floor and in the first floor living area.

Dermot Bannon Architects/Enda Cavanagh

FKL Architects/Verena Hilgenfeld

Dermot Bannon Architects

People think double-height spaces are a waste of valuable floor area, but in this case we didn't lose any because it was in a new extension. It solved all of the problems in the house, which had amazing views of the sea from the front. The owners wanted a better connection with the garden, as they lived in the back of the house, where a scullery led to the exterior. They always felt this was a poor relation in comparison to the front of the house, so we balanced this – instead of dramatic views, there was a dramatic space. And with the added light and double-height space, we brought drama to the whole house.

FORM DENOTES FUNCTION

A variety of heights can denote various functions in a home. Higher ceilings tend to be in more formal spaces, where there are large gatherings. A place for smaller gatherings, perhaps six people around a table for dinner, should have a lower ceiling, making the space more intimate.

If you sit beside someone in a place with high ceilings, such as a church, with the acoustics bouncing the sound around, you can feel farther

away from them than you would if you were sitting at the same distance from them in a small snug in a pub. In the same way, you can feel closer to people in a small gathering beneath a lower ceiling. If the ceiling is lowered, even to less than the standard 2.4 metres, over a tiny table, you can create a snug. In Irish houses we traditionally had cosy, intimate spaces, such as nooks around a fireplace, that feel private and intimate. That's why in grand houses with 12-foot-high ceilings they sometimes put in four-poster beds, with their solid roofs and suspended fabric, to create a more intimate space: a room within a room.

People often think architecture is about opening up spaces, but it is a mix of the two: open and enclosed. Architects Edwin Lutyens and Charles Voysey could open up spaces, as they did in the substantial country houses they designed, but they also used window seats and alcoves to create more intimate areas. In their Blackwood Golf Centre in County Down, architects O'Donnell + Tuomey created booths beneath a lowered ceiling. Charles Rennie Mackintosh's high-backed chairs were used by ladies who lunch to pull the chairs into the table, creating a circular wall behind them – an enclosure to gossip in.

When extending or converting homes, you usually have a set ceiling height to deal with. In the practice we often address this when putting a kitchen onto a big, majestic living room by lowering the floor of the extension.

Garbhan Doran Architects

TURN UP THE VOLUME

....

We tend to think of a room's length and breadth as its volume, but the height should be considered too. There should be a direct relationship between the dimension of the room and the height, as in Georgian houses. Sometimes when people create a huge extension but keep the ceiling height at 8 feet, it can feel as if the ceiling is coming in on top of you.

Modern developers never look at the ceiling height as part of the volume – they build an 8-foot-high ceiling and that's it – yet it is incredibly important to how a space feels.

CHAPTER 3

MAKING YOUR HOME WORK FOR YOU

ONE BIG HAPPY FAMILY

....

Houses in Ireland, England and across Europe were traditionally built for extended families because human beings are designed to live communally. The idea of the single-unit family living in one house is a 20th-century one. As a society, we have segregated ourselves from our communities and in our homes.

Previously, three generations of a family lived together – and they still do in some countries. It works both practically – grandparents looking after grandchildren, adult children looking after parents – and to satisfy the needs of the human psyche.

Aughey O'Flaherty Architects/Marie-Louise Halpenny

Dermot Bannon Architects/Ros Kavanagh

Psychologists have found that loneliness and a fear of being alone can lead to addictions, anxiety disorders, sleeplessness and even illness (although we all need to be alone sometimes, which is different from feeling lonely). One of the harshest punishments in prison is solitary confinement.

If two parents and their children live in isolation, there is no one to turn to if there is discord. If you live communally, then when you have a row or a problem, other generations and people who know

Amanda Bone Architects/Ros Kavanagh

THE HEART, THE HEAD, THE GUT

······························

Irish architect Ross Cahill-O'Brien, who I once worked with, gave a lecture while I was in college in which he said every home should have a heart, a head and a gut. He designed and named the Kitchen nightclub, beneath Dublin's Clarence Hotel, which was a gut, the bowel of the hotel, with water running through it via curved 'arteries'.

Communal spaces are the heart of a home – the kitchen, living and dining spaces. The head part of a home is for headspace: the private rooms

the situation can help sort things out. If elderly people live on their own, they should live in smaller communities where they can leave their door open.

The idea of a single-family house in Ireland took hold in the 1950s and 1960s, and yet we still inherently crave community. Because communal living can offer a depth and richness in life, I see my main job as creating communal spaces. This goes against the developer-led or Victorian model of houses with segregated rooms.

People spend most of their time in the kitchen, and yet kitchens are now quite small in Irish houses. Kitchens are perfect for communal activities because eating and cooking bind people together, from sitting down to meals to gathering around someone who is cooking for an informal chat. It's analogous to the water cooler moment at work, allowing for informal conversations in a communal space, with people moving on and others coming in. It's very different from the forced formality of talking in a sitting room.

Dermot Bannon Architect

Sterin O'Shea Architects

we all need to retreat to. These include a study, a bedroom or a sitting room that becomes a den.

The gut is the working areas – utility, storage, boot rooms, laundries, drying room, bins, machines – the things we tend to overlook. About 10 per cent of homes should be for storage. Even big 4,000-square-foot houses have tiny rooms to accommodate these working areas.

For example, I like to include separate boot rooms in my designs for muddy items being brought in from outside, such as buggies, clothes or bicycles. Or with people often travelling far afield for work, it is worth finding somewhere for suitcases other than the attic, or at least creating easy access to the attic.

You also need a good place to dry clothes with all the rain we have here. In the past, if people were

at home all day, someone would have been able to get the clothes in from the line when it rains, but that is not possible if everyone is out working. This needs to be planned, otherwise visitors coming in

Dermot Bannon Architects/Enda Cavanagh

the back door could well be treated to the sight of your smalls drying, or that lovely open-plan space you created could have a clothes horse permanently in one corner.

FAMILY HOUSE
....

Instead of clearly defined private realms and communal spaces, houses often have rooms that are neither one nor the other: children frequently play in bedrooms and the dining room can be largely unused.

If the spaces in a home are arranged in a sequence of public to private, it feels right. That awkward feeling you get in an open-plan office when you walk past cubicles in which people are working in order to reach a conference room at the back is the same in a house. The entrance should be in a very public space; you shouldn't enter past bedrooms. That is why having living rooms at the front of the house did work once – they were placed to one side beyond the front door so that a local priest or formal guest could visit without going into the communal family spaces.

But most Irish people love to use the back door. In my granny's old farmhouse, everyone drove into the farmyard and went straight into the kitchen through the back door. Formal visitors would come in the main drive and enter through the front door into the parlour. This was so rarely used that one day a visitor called to the front door and couldn't open it because it had been painted shut and nobody had even realised it because people never came in that way.

Donaghy & Dimond Architects

Dermot Bannon Architects

As a nation we go straight into the kitchen via the back door. That's why Irish houses don't work any more. Because people want to walk straight into the kitchen, we need to reassess how we live in our houses. Nowadays, if we meet people formally, we frequently do so outside the home, while informal visitors to a home often feel so comfortable that they will help themselves to a cup of tea or coffee and homeowners have no issue with that. The formality has gone out of homes and is irrelevant for the 21st century. We are moving back to the recognition that we are not solitary beings.

TURNAROUND

When setting out a house, make sure people enter straight into a kitchen or living space. Next come the more private or semi-private areas, such as a den for kids, and then the bedrooms are further back again. The corridors that connect them

should be celebrated spaces, not the segregated areas we have become used to, such as the long, dark corridors in bungalows and spec houses. The worst examples are those awful corridors in chain hotels with no windows, no view and no seat, running past bedroom after bedroom and feeling a mile long.

The corridor needs to be the artery of a home. If you just think of it as a utilitarian circulation space, it's a waste. In Georgian houses you can see how the living spaces connect in a loop, with the corridor to one side and double doors between rooms. The hall and corridor should have windows and be wide enough for furniture so that they are a pleasure to use as opposed to a place to be quickly passed through. If you put a seat in a corridor – and in old country houses there is often a window seat in a corridor, making it a joy to use – you are back to that water-cooler moment, where children interact, people chat or you can read a book.

PG Architects/Peter Cook

DESIGN FOR
YOUR LIFE

·······································

When planning your home, ignore preconceptions or what the neighbours have. As the late Steve Jobs of Apple said, never give people what they think they want. He believed that market research only tells you what people already have. He said, 'It's really hard to design products by focus groups. A lot of times, people don't know what they want until you show it to them.' A house should be for *your* life, not your neighbour's life or your forebears' lives.

You can focus on this by writing a list of what you do during the day, what rooms you use and in what order. A Venn diagram (circles that interlink) will show how rooms interact, and the bigger the circle, the more you use a room. The overlaps will show which rooms share parts of their use and will help you decipher how you use your home.

You might find that you don't use a formal dining space and instead use a small kitchen 95 per cent of the time, cramming a table and chairs into the space. Or you may find that you only use a big

living room 5 per cent of the time and you might decide that little-used rooms can be changed to have a dual function, such as becoming a playroom or office for some of the time.

The Swiss/French architect Le Corbusier said a house is a machine for living in. That sounds slightly brutal, but they are there to facilitate life. A properly designed house with a heart, a head and a gut is the perfect machine for living in.

Ailtireacht)

CHAPTER 4

THE STUFF THAT HOMES ARE MADE OF

Choosing materials is the part of the build that the client gets very involved with. When it comes to the structure of the build, clients feel that someone else is dealing with it – which they will be – but materials are the things that they will see and feel every day. Architects are happy to choose materials too, but it is not your home unless you are involved in the process and love them.

I find that it helps to be methodical and to work in a certain order, otherwise it can feel daunting. You don't want to be walking aimlessly through showrooms full of products and colours, feeling overwhelmed by choice.

Garbhan Doran Architects

WINDOWS

Start with the windows, which is a hugely expensive package that can be up to a third of the cost of a building project. It is worth getting involved in choosing these, as they will set the tone for the rest of the materials choices. Obviously they have an external finish, but there is also an internal one that needs to be considered too.

Darmody Barnard Architects/Enda Cavanagh

ALUCLAD WINDOWS

If your budget allows, Aluclad timber is the best. It has all the warmth of timber inside with aluminium cladding outside, which needs little or no maintenance. You can choose any colour you like outside and you can change the finish inside by varnishing or painting the wood. You can choose a hardwood or softwood inside. Hardwood is from a more slow-growing tree, while softwood is from speedier growers, such as pine. They are often more knotted.

If you leave the wood exposed, it will, or should, influence the choice of joinery and other materials in the house, such as flooring and shelving. If you are painting the wood, choose something neutral rather than a

Aughey O'Flaherty Architects/Marie-Louise Halpenny

definite colour; you don't necessarily want to have to repaint the windows each time you repaint the house.

TIMBER WINDOWS

These have timber on both the inside and outside, so unlike Aluclad windows, the external surface will need to be repainted periodically.

Peter Legge Associates

ALUMINIUM WINDOWS

These have aluminium on both the inside and outside and come in almost any colour. Choose wisely: greys, blacks and neutrals are best, providing a calm backdrop to a room. The colour is not that easy to change because you will need to re-spray the window.

PVC WINDOWS

This is an inexpensive option and contemporary PVC windows can achieve good U-values (they cut heat loss). They are not the most environmentally friendly option, however, as they are not as easy to replace.

FLOORS

Once the windows have been chosen, flooring is the next in line.

TIMBER

I love a timber floor in our Irish climate. In fact, my preference is to have timber everywhere, even in the kitchen, for its warmth and tactility. Yet lots of people have tiles throughout their homes, something I feel is better suited to warmer climates. It is easy to be seduced by them in swanky showrooms, in reams of glistening white or creams, but I wonder at how practical they are here, even in a well-insulated home. There is just something nice about a hardwood floor.

If you have wooden window frames, then match the floor to them. If the window has been painted, then you have free rein on the floor.

Hardwoods, from slow-growing trees, are denser and age well in a home. They can range in tone from light oak to dark walnut (make sure you buy them from a sustainable source: supplies are limited in the world). They are usually more expensive than softwood, but the latter is also good for flooring. A lot of older houses will have pine (softwood) floors, so you will want to match this in an extension. Because older pine will have gradually darkened, you can stain newer pine to match it.

While the words *hardwood* and *softwood* don't necessarily describe the wood's consistency, softwood can be softer. Heels, for instance, will damage it, so it can look more rough-and-tumble with age, but that's the patina of life.

In period houses, the wooden floors were designed to be covered up. The trend now is to pull up carpets, but if the floorboards are not in great condition, don't go to the ends of the earth to salvage them. It might even be worth putting new hardwood floors down.

Whatever timber you pick for the floor, do carry it through to the joinery in the rest of your home (doors, shelves and so on).

SOLID TIMBER FLOORS

Most people aspire to a floor that has timber all the way through, and they can look amazing. Normally they fit together with tongue-and-groove joints, so you don't need – or see – nails. One disadvantage is that unless the timber has become acclimatised and cleared of moisture, it can cup a bit and warp. Ask about this when buying. One way to help stop warping is to bond it directly to the floor.

SEMI-SOLID ENGINEERED BOARD

This typically comprises two layers: one of solid timber and another material such as plywood or softwood on the underside, running in a different direction to the top grain. This strengthens and stabilises the flooring, making it less likely to cup or warp. A good engineered floor can be more expensive than a solid floor. While some people feel that a solid floor can be sanded more often, it can only go as deep as the tongue-and-groove, so semi-solid floors can usually be sanded just as much.

PARQUET FLOORS

These puzzle-like pieces of solid timber, recalling French chateaux and school halls, are typically glued directly to the floor and can be laid in beautiful patterns, such as herringbone.

LAMINATED FLOORS

Made of synthetic materials, such as MDF with a thin veneer of melamine bearing an image of timber, laminated floors are inexpensive and can offer a good quick fix, perhaps for a bedroom or playroom. It won't last as long as timber and it can feel and sound different underfoot.

Lawrence and Long Architects/Marie-Louise Halpenny

John Feely Architects/Ros Kavanagh

STONE

You can't beat stone. It comes in amazing colours and textures and can be carried through from floors to worktops, bathrooms and kitchens.

When choosing a stone floor it is important to see a lot of it in a space. Things that look garish close up can look good in a large area. When we were choosing tiles for a part of Dublin Airport, someone brought in a sample tile that looked busy, but in big areas it looked really good.

Expect colour changes and shading through stone tile, which is okay. It's a natural material and it formed that way: allow it to be like that.

Consider taking whatever you put on floors up the walls. People might think that's boring, but bathrooms, for instance, can be very busy places, with lots of towels and products, so it's good to have a calm backdrop.

GRANITE

A lot of granite in Ireland is really hard and strong, making it great for floors, worktops and walls. It typically comes in greys and blacks, but you can also get brown, speckled versions. I like it in its natural, unpolished state; when polished it can be quite speckled. Certain stones suit polishing and some don't.

LIMESTONE

Available in lots of light colours, including creams and greys, limestone makes an amazing floor, either polished or unpolished. Limestone has a great texture and you will always find hidden secrets within it, such as fossils. Some limestone can be porous and will need to be sealed, so ask your supplier for advice.

MARBLE

Marble comes in a huge range of textures and colours and it can look great either unpolished or polished. Ask your supplier whether it needs to be sealed – white marble is renowned for picking up red wine rings from glasses placed on kitchen countertops.

SLATE

Slate comes in naturally thinner slices and is a great floor finish. Don't be afraid of using its darker tones of grey and black on floors, and consider complementing that with bright walls.

CONCRETE AND TERRAZZO

Mention concrete and it sends a shiver up many a spine, being associated with brutal, hard, 1960s architecture. Yet polished concrete can have associations with walking on a beach because the stones in the aggregate are sliced during the polishing process. You can choose the colour of the stones, from white to sandy to dark grey, as well as the colour of the concrete, from pale to dark. If you choose the right dye against the right aggregate, you get an absolutely beautiful floor, something I can stare at for ages.

Terrazzo contains more chippings, from marble to glass. Its links with institutional use in schools and hospitals can put some people off, but it can be lovely, say, in great colours running across the floor and turned up the wall.

Donal Coffey/Alice Clancy

TILES

Tiles are cheaper than stone and come in an amazing array of colours. Pick something that works with the floor and windows and aim for neutral colours.

There are two types of tile: ceramic and porcelain. Ceramic tiles have the colour on the top surface, while porcelain generally has the colour going all through it. Porcelain is more hard-wearing, so if your budget allows, it is the better option. To avoid using a lot of grout, choose a sharp-edged tile that can be pushed up against others, allowing for a smaller gap and a better look.

The advantage of a tile over stone is that you can pick one with a specific slip resistance. But be wary of something that is too slip resistant, as its greater roughness can make it hang on to dirt more stubbornly.

MOSAIC TILES

The small size of mosaic tiles can make bathrooms look much bigger. In the case of mosaic, the grout can become part of the whole look, becoming a web. Mosaic on a worktop can be a bad idea though, as worn grout is up closer to your eyes.

Mosaic is a flexible option for wet rooms that slope to a drainage point, as they easily bend with a floor's contours.

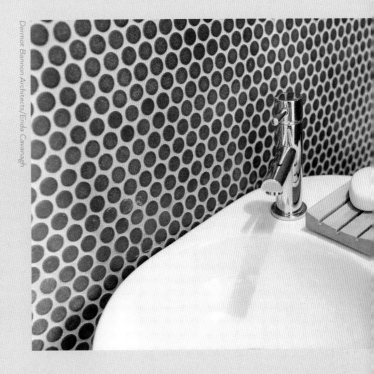

Dermot Bannon Architects/Enda Cavanagh

LINO AND RUBBER

These other natural options take flooring to a whole new realm with their huge array of colours and even images.

JOINERY

This is the next part of your overall palette and it needs to be tied in with the windows and flooring. These items include shelving, window seats, doors, frames, wardrobes, etc.

KITCHEN WORKTOPS

Having chosen your windows and floors, take samples to the kitchen showroom so you won't risk being seduced by a showroom model that looks amazing but wouldn't work in your home.

Opt for neutral tones that will help the kitchen sit in the background of a room, unless you really want to make a statement in, say, orange or blue. Think about this decision carefully, though, as colours can date.

Choose something that works with the floor. As a general guide, consider having all horizontal surfaces (worktops, tiles, etc.) working together and all vertical surfaces like doors and cabinets working with each other.

See Chapter 8 for more on kitchen worktops.

STONE WORKTOPS

Stone makes a durable surface with a coolness loved by pastry chefs. It may need to be sealed.

QUARTZ WORKTOPS

This is a coloured concrete with stone aggregate running through it. It comes in an amazing colour range, from white to black and greys and browns in between. Tying in well with a floor, this can look stunning and is really durable.

TIMBER WORKTOPS

This looks beautiful but needs care, as it can become damaged around sinks and beneath heavy wear and tear. It needs a bit of maintenance, such as oiling, so if you are not prepared to do this, choose stone or quartz.

LAMINATE WORKTOPS

Available in synthetic materials such as Formica and melamine, it is best to be true to this by choosing a solid colour rather than one that emulates a natural material such as wood or stone.

Sterrin O'Shea Architects

PAINT COLOURS

Put all of the materials in your home together on a mood board and introduce different paint colours into this to see what suits.

Once you have chosen your colours, create samples and see what works in different rooms. North, south, east and west aspects can throw such a different light on paint that it can look completely different, meaning that a colour that works in one half of the house won't work in another.

Peter Legge Associates

FURNISHINGS

The neutral backdrop should continue with any carpets and curtains – greys work really well in an Irish climate – as you don't want to have to replace these too often. They will have a longer life if they are plain; trends or personal favourites can be added with cushions and other, less permanent pieces.

When choosing paintings, lamps and so on, forget the overall palette – this is one area in which you don't want to become part of a whole package. Each item should be true to you. Have the things you really want around you, things that mean something to you and are part of your journey through life.

Your home should reflect everything about you and your family. If your kids do really brightly coloured painting (or if you do), they don't need to be in any stylised order on the walls. It just shows it's a house with artistic and creative people in it – and the house allows that.

OUTDOOR MATERIALS

Amanda Bone Architects/Ros Kavanagh

Before we had the ability to import huge quantities of building materials, we built houses from what the Irish landscape had to offer, and even now those elements will make a house sit beautifully in the surrounding land. The landscape and local area provide the palette of materials best suited to building a house in the countryside, so look to that for cues of what to use. You could even try to just use materials that would be available within a couple of miles. The local stone our forebears built with was usually covered with render, so a building finished in this way, with a render true to tradition, will sit well in the Irish landscape.

When renovating a traditional home, be wary of stripping it back to its stone, because they were often constructed from inferior stone – or 'rubble' – that was not meant to be exposed. It could make the building

more vulnerable to the weather and water penetration. Thick cut-stone was typically used in grander buildings, such as churches and manors.

If you do introduce a contrasting material, then do it with a purpose. I hate feature walls and prefer a larger expanse, such as a complete elevation or a wing, in stone or brick or timber. This references old farms, in which the house might be rendered while a nearby barn would be in stone. If opting for exposed stone, use one that is indigenous to the area. Be wary of using an 'alien' stone as a contrast material, such as local limestone with imported sandstone.

Peter Legge Associates

BRICK

While indigenous brick sits well in the landscape, very few areas of Ireland fire clay to make brick. In these places it can be a good option, but all too often you see 1970s buildings made from inappropriate brick that doesn't tie in with the landscape.

TIMBER

A good hardwood such as cedar or iroko, ensuring that it is not endangered, can be used to create an external skin to a building. If left untreated, it turns a silvery grey that blends into the landscape very well.

FIBRE CEMENT PANELS

This contemporary material, put on the outside of buildings, works well in the colours of the land: greys, blacks, dark brown. For this reason, don't pick colours from a brochure, but take sample panels out into the countryside and match them with nature.

SLATE AND METAL

In roofs, natural slate sits best in the Irish landscape. But you can have more contemporary additions to the roof, perhaps in lower-pitched sections, in natural zinc or copper.

CITY HOUSES

People building new houses or extensions in the city have all sorts of references to pick up on, as towns are a big melting pot of materials, from stone to brick. It does change from one area to the next, with suburbs typically having more brick and seaside homes being rendered. To fit in with this, look around at other buildings. Yours does not have to be the same, but work with the context and try to fit in, in your own way.

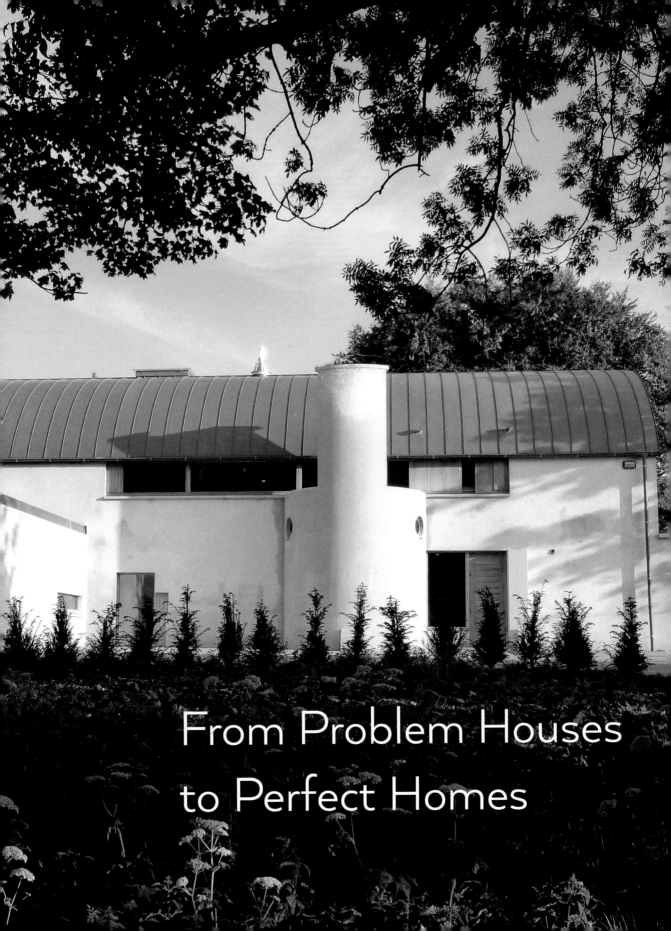

From Problem Houses
to Perfect Homes

CHAPTER 5

SOLVING DESIGN ISSUES

Until about a century ago, country homes in rural Ireland were mainly small cottages and vernacular farmhouses. And yet the houses built in the latter part of the 20th century didn't stem from these homes because Ireland didn't have a house typology that could evolve. Cottages tended to have minimum dimensions, with a central fire heating it, while farmhouses were typically one room deep and proved difficult to renovate when people sought to upgrade and upsize when there was more money around from the 1950s onwards. At that time we didn't have the technology to insulate the farmhouses, so damp was also an issue.

So even though these cottages and farmhouses were beautiful to look at, Irish people turned their backs on them during the 1950s, 60s and 70s. Instead, this era saw the rise of the bungalow as the solution chosen by those with their own plot of land in the countryside. This generation disregarded so much of what rural Ireland had been architecturally.

After Independence, Ireland went through massive change and rejected what it saw as the English Georgian house (although technically, Georgian architecture stems from classical architecture in Italy and Greece and was a pan-European style – it's just that the British version was named after the monarchy). This can be seen in the destruction

FKL Architects/Ros Kavanagh

of 12 Georgian buildings in the middle of Fitzwilliam Street in Dublin (which had been the longest Georgian street in Dublin) to make way for new ESB offices in the 1960s.

People embraced the end of rule from London, and in a country that had many landlords and landowners from the UK, they wanted to claim back the land. There was a massive revolt against everything that had gone before, yet there was no new style to base the future on. While in Dublin, Limerick and Cork there were strong house typologies in the form of Georgian and Victorian homes, there was little to go on in the countryside.

BUNGALOW BLIGHT

In answer to people's yearning for a new way of building now that they could afford to construct a home, along came books on bungalows. The most famous was *Bungalow Bliss* by Jack Fitzsimons, but there were others, such as *The Irish Bungalow Book* by Ted McCarthy. These provided a catalogue of homes that people could pick from and plans to give to their builders. While the homes looked different on the outside, they were all quite similar inside, and this is where the problems started.

In looking back to the traditional farmhouses, it is obvious that the people who built them understood the land. They knew where the sun was and where shelter could be found, and they positioned the houses to benefit from these. My granny's farmhouse had no windows on the north side to protect occupants from harsh weather. This respect for the surroundings explains why older houses seem to be more rooted in the countryside and belong there. This sense of being rooted is also helped by the fact that the houses nestle into the land, are often surrounded by trees and, unlike many new homes in the country, are not built at the highest part of the site.

The arrival of the bungalow books disconnected us because they took a one-size-fits-all approach (although to be fair on Jack Fitzsimons, in his book he did explain the importance of siting and setting and he reproduced the Landscape Amenity Checklist contained in *Planning for Amenity, Recreation and Tourism*, published by An Foras Forbartha). The house design was taken out of the book and just plonked onto any site, as if by helicopter (or large sections of them anyway).

The books made the houses easy and quick to design and build, but that came at a price, which was a severance of an understanding of, and connection with, the land. The bungalow designers and builders just didn't consider the views/ windows, sheltered aspects, orientation and so on. What's more, the houses always faced the road, wherever that happened to be.

The disconnect happened with materials too. In the past the houses would have been built with stone and timber from the surrounding land, often from within a mile radius. But bungalows were made from fake stone and plaster rather than indigenous materials, which severed the connection with the land in another way.

So what we have are houses that were built without knowledge of the land, and in 90 per cent of cases, without the use of an architect.

Aughey O'Flaherty Architects/Paul Tierney

MAYO MEETS THE MEDITERRANEAN

Package holidays grew in popularity in the 1970s, at the same time that people had more money to build their own homes with. Some of the foreign motifs travelled back to Ireland, so we got Spanish-style villas, with big arches within, in Leitrim and Cavan.

As fewer people were surrounded by traditional cottages and farmhouses, there was a knock-on effect. The new style became the one to follow across the country, without being tied to any part of Ireland's geography, culture or history. Wherever you go, the houses are the same.

Instead of completely rethinking the design, most of us think that the bungalow is the Irish house typology and that these are what we must build. Why? Because it is the only thing that can be seen.

DORMANT DORMERS

While this house type is very difficult to adapt, it did evolve in the only way it could – into a dormer bungalow – in an effort to extend upwards without technically adding another floor. Thus, a bungalow can be top heavy, comprised of one-third walls to two-thirds roof, while a traditional farmhouse is the inverse of that.

Yet a dormer bungalow can actually be higher than a two-storey house because 8-foot-high ceilings have to be created in order to bury an upstairs room into the roof. If you see a dormer bungalow and a two-storey farmhouse beside each other, you will often find that they are the same height.

Peter Legge Associates

Sterrin O'Shea Architects

We redesigned a two-storey house on a beautiful site overlooking the River Shannon. The existing house was two rooms deep and centred around a corridor, while the roof had been made higher so that bedrooms could be fitted into it. There was a lot of wasted space. We started from scratch and built them a two-storey home that was actually lower than the dormer bungalow it replaced.

Yet people still think that they won't get planning permission for a two-storey house in the country, so they turn up in the planning office with plans for a dormer bungalow because they think it is the only type of house the planners will allow.

The good news is that many planners now issue guidelines with a big X crossed through dormer bungalows and inappropriate designs. They are seeking something that will sit in the landscape better, and many local authorities right across Ireland have produced Rural Design Guides (PDFs can be downloaded from local authority websites).

PROBLEMS – AND SOLUTIONS

A bungalow is not necessarily a building that should be overlooked – they can be changed to suit contemporary life.

PROBLEMS

1. ASPECT

The houses in bungalow books have a very similar layout to each other, with a living room at the front, a kitchen/dining room at the back with a utility room, a bathroom to the back, either left or right, and a bedroom wing, with bedrooms to the front and back. And the front door

always faces the road, regardless of the aspect. It surprises me how many people haven't a clue where the south – and sun – is, so they could spend their lives living in the cold north side of a home without much sunlight.

2. OUTSIDE SPACE

Bungalows are generally single-volume rectangles, like a shoebox, which leaves them exposed to all the wind we have in Ireland. There is no sheltered spot to sit in outside, no enclosed outdoor 'room'.

3. ROOM SIZE

In Ireland we became obsessed with the number of rooms in a house, and bungalow designs often squeeze in so many rooms that the size of each one is very small. This was compounded by a grant that was available for houses under a certain size, creating lots of small rooms as opposed to larger, more comfortable spaces. Four-bedroom bungalows built in the 1970s are probably only equivalent to a three-bedroom house built now.

Dermot Bannon Architects

4. KITCHEN

The kitchen and dining rooms were put at the back of the house, regardless of where the views were. Even though people tend to live in kitchens and dining areas the most, these were tiny – too small to hold a whole family despite the fact that it was the space in which they all gathered. The formal dining room, on the other hand, tended to be unused and so it would be wasted if it was placed on the south side of the house.

The typology has not changed since the 1970s. There was a huge disconnect, and this included a formal living room to the front of the house, kept as a 'good' room that was used only at weekends or on special occasions such as Christmas and Easter. Such rooms are irrelevant today. The inefficient design of these houses meant there was an awful lot of wasted space.

Ryan Kenihan Architects/Alice Clancy

5. CORRIDORS

Old farmhouses were typically one room deep and had a lot of circulation space with windows, whereas bungalows tend to be two rooms deep, necessitating long, dark, narrow corridors, like those you find in some chain hotels.

Donaghy & Dimond Architects/Philip Lauterbach

Sterrin O'Shea Architects

7. UTILITY ROOM

This is my bugbear in houses. As a nation, we use the back door and generally have tiny utility rooms beside it. Lots of Irish families had a back kitchen and the Irish utility room evolved from this, as it was felt necessary to have it beside the kitchen and the back door. Thus, generations have walked through the utility space – where families would often hang their clothes to dry – on the way into a house.

6. STORAGE

Storage space was often neglected in bungalows, where the object was to cram in as many rooms as possible – for instance, four bedrooms with en suites, a kitchen/dining room, living room and bathroom – so all of the space was used up and ancillary spaces were omitted. This resulted in big houses on huge plots of land that had nowhere to store shopping bags and Christmas decorations.

Aughey O'Flaherty Architects/Paul Tierney

8. RUNNING THE M50 AROUND A HOUSE

People often feel it is necessary to be able to drive to the front and back doors of their home and so they run a road right around it to facilitate that. But it means that the opportunity for any nice outside space has been lost.

SOLUTIONS

1. ASPECT

When redesigning a home, find out where south is and place the important rooms you spend much of the day in on that side of the house (see Chapter 2 on natural light).

Aughey O'Flaherty Architects/Grand Designs

Peter Legge Associates

2. OUTSIDE SPACE

If you are extending onto a bungalow, try to put the new part perpendicular to the old – making an L-shaped or T-shaped building – so that you create a garden 'room', giving you a corner to back into, something that all humans like. Find out where the suntrap is and use the building and extension to capture that.

PG Architects/Peter Cook

3. ROOM SIZE

If you are extending a bungalow, don't automatically think that the new part should be a kitchen and living space. Instead, knock the existing kitchen and formal dining room together: it's a room that has always asked for this to be done. Even better, if there is a living room at the front (and then a dining room and kitchen), consider knocking all three rooms together. Otherwise, think about turning part of the space into a TV den or office: make it useful.

Ideally a bedroom will then go into the new extension. This will allow you to increase the size of the bedrooms in the existing house by knocking them through. For instance, you can turn an existing four-bedroom bungalow into a three-bedroom home by knocking two bedrooms through and then adding a fourth bedroom back in through the extension.

Aughey O'Flaherty Architects/Marie-Louise Halpenny

Peter Legge Associates

4. CORRIDOR

Dark, internal corridors are the most miserable places on earth: you have no idea where you are and no connection to the outside. Try to introduce natural light into the space, either via a rooflight (if that's the only way) or by creating a window. If there's a wardrobe backing onto an en suite at the end of the corridor, for instance, there could be a way to knock this through.

In a house we worked on in Tipperary, we took out an en suite and put in a large window and window seat that overlooks shrubs and trees. By opening up the corridor like this, we put some soul back into the house.

Dermot Bannon Architects

5. UTILITY

If the utility room is near the kitchen, by the back door, as it often is in a bungalow, this could be turned into some kind of boot room. If you use the back door a lot, then it is the perfect place to offload and store all of your outside gear: Wellies, buggies, scooters, coats and so on. Move the utility room to a more useful place, near the bedrooms and bathroom, which is a better location for laundry.

6. M50 AROUND THE HOUSE

Something has to give here. It's not all about the car – the connection between the home and outside space is far more important. A dedicated parking spot

should be designed to one side of the house. If the home is L-shaped or T-shaped, with a courtyard, cars must be kept out of this to allow a connection with the garden and views, and for patios. I think eating, reading and chatting outside is much more conducive to a good quality of life than being able to drive to the door.

Steve Larkin Architects/Alice Clancy

Donaghy & Dimond Architects

CHAPTER 6

EXTENDING YOUR HORIZONS

An extension usually adds value to a house, but a poorly built one will detract from it because new buyers will mentally add in the cost of pulling it down. Sometimes a badly designed extension can even leave a house (which may in itself be in good shape) in a worse state than it was before. A well-designed extension, on the other hand, can make a whole house work and will negate the need for people to move to another home.

For a long time we constructed the same type of (badly built) extensions in Ireland. Generally a builder would come along and just construct something he'd done before. This is nothing against builders or clients – it's just the way it evolved.

Houses were often extended poorly and destroyed the rooms behind them in the existing house. For instance, the main type of extension is a kitchen, and this addition would just be a bigger version of what was beside it without addressing issues of light or function and so on; all they did was add more floor space. The room to which the extension was added was often relegated to a go-between place that you had to walk through to get to the extension.

I usually start by stripping back any existing bad extension when it doesn't work for the client. People extend when they are under pressure for space, perhaps as a family grows or family members move in. Often they are in a hurry and

Ryan Kennihan Architects/Alice Clancy

say they don't care where, or what, it is – they just need the space. This lack of planning is often evident when I come along and they tell me they are not happy with it and wish they had done it differently. It served us at the time, they often tell me, but now we can't live in it; it's dark and it doesn't function.

Yet people can spend €20,000 to €40,000 on such 'temporary' extensions. They are throwing money away that could have been spent doing something properly in the first place, and it may not have cost anywhere near that figure.

WHERE TO START

···

When I meet clients for the first time, I find
that some of the biggest problems for people
who have lived in a home for 10, 20 or 30 years
is that they can't see the wood for the trees.
Sometimes people are so caught up with the
existing structure and rooms and decide that all
the things that are wrong with it can be solved by
an extension, yet half of the work might need to
be done to the existing house.

I get them to draw up a wish list, and seeing the
house as a blank canvas, I sketch up the property
and don't put any room names on the layout.
Then I look at reconfiguring the house, putting
rooms where they need to be. They might want a
kitchen at the back of the house, but architectural
principles may mean that the kitchen should be at
the front. I identify problems and look for missed

opportunities. After allocating rooms in the existing house for maximum use, I then see how much of an extension is needed.

I get them to see it all with fresh eyes, looking at where the views are and where the sunlight is (and that old problem of having a disused dining room flooded with sun). There is no point adding an extension if there are existing rooms whose potential has not been unlocked. If there are rooms in the house that don't work well, now is the time to address this.

Looking at your lifestyle and what you require gives you the chance to design around your needs and put your stamp on the house; there is no point in making it identical to your neighbour's home because you and your lifestyle are not the same.

WHERE TO EXTEND

Adding an extension is not simply a matter of adding a structure. You need to consider how to integrate it with the rest of the house – what it plugs into, how it connects and designing it to make the rest of the house function better.

The easiest and most popular way of extending is a single-storey structure in the back garden. It is very difficult to extend to the front. Generally the garden is smaller, it provides vehicle access and you won't be able to change the façade in a conservation area. Lots of things inhibit it, and if you do extend to the front, it is usually a smaller structure.

If the extension isn't big, then it is an exempted development – meaning you don't need planning permission (see Chapter 14 for more on planning permission).

FKL Architects/Paul Tierney

Another easy way to extend is by converting a structure that is already there, such as a garage or shed. If it is not attached to the house, look at integrating an outbuilding into the overall plan to create a courtyard. This could be an old cowhouse that has been made redundant through modern farming methods – perhaps the new tractor doesn't fit into it – and so it ends up acting as a glorified shed. But it could make a lovely extension, with its high ceilings and lofty spaces.

Donaghy & Dimond Architects/Marie-Louise Halpenny

EXTENDING TO THE SOUTH

If you are lucky enough to have a south-facing rear garden, you have hit the jackpot. This orientation is best for light and sun, so it is great for connecting to the garden: you can throw open the back doors and spill out. Most extensions are carved out to solve the problem that is inherent in many Irish houses, which is to have a better family space, so a south-facing extension is the perfect location for a kitchen/dining room.

South-facing rooms with lots of glass do tend to overheat in the summer, though, so it's a good idea to design in an overhang – a *brise soleil*. If you put this at the right height it will shade the glass from high summer sun while letting in low winter sun. Also bear in mind that south-facing light will penetrate into a building for up to 6 metres, so if you are extending further than that you may have to supplement the light stream with a rooflight, a further window or even a courtyard (see Chapter 7 on courtyards).

Ryan Kennihan Architects/Alice Clancy

EXTENDING TO THE NORTH

Light from this direction is trickier, although more consistent than southern light. Think carefully before deciding on huge amounts of glass, because this is the coldest wall on the house and you have a greater chance of losing energy. That said, glass technology has vastly improved and if you opt for glass with a low U-value (the U stands for unit heat loss and it measures the amount of heat that passes through a material), you can put in large areas of glazing facing north. It is certainly worth it if you have a lovely view or garden.

A problem with the northern aspect is getting enough natural light into the space. It helps to supplement any lack with a rooflight. The way to work out where to place this is to find the point where the sun comes over the roof. Stand in the

Ryan Kennihan Architects/Alice Clancy

EXTENDING TO THE EAST

If your garden faces east, you will be treated to sun in the morning, but by 11am or midday it may have gone. It's worth aiming for a dual aspect, connecting the house all the way through to a west window. Then you will get evening sun too. Or you could create a linear extension running perpendicular to the main house to gather light for longer.

Gatbhan Doran Architects

back garden and find the spot where the sun hits you in the face – you may need to stand on a chair or something higher to get to ceiling height. Where the sun clears the shadow line of the building shows you where to position the rooflight.

There are advantages to a northern aspect. One is that you can put plants right up against the building without worrying about shading them from the sun. Northern light is also a consistent light, which is why you'll find that rooflights in places such as hospitals, airports, swimming pools and art galleries are angled to the north – to provide natural light without anyone getting sun gleaming in their face, which isn't fun if you are sitting at a reception desk and can't move. Many artists prefer to work in northern light because of its cool colour and consistency.

EXTENDING TO THE WEST

This would suit people who are working elsewhere all day and use the garden later in the day. Adults tend to use gardens from 4pm onwards, whereas children are in them at all times. If a west-facing extension is a living room, it's a perfect place to be in later in the day to capture the last of the evening sun. If it's not dual aspect, you will miss the morning sun and it will be worth putting a rooflight in if you can.

STRUCTURE AND THE EXISTING HOUSE

A key inhibitor to most extensions, which often benefit from an opening out of rooms, is that people assume there are structural walls that cannot be moved. That's not necessarily true. While non-structural walls simply divide rooms, structural walls support the house above: the ceiling, floor above and an upstairs wall, or all three and beyond.

An easy way to find out which walls are structural is to first knock on them – if it sounds hollow, it's probably a stud wall that is not load bearing (although some stud walls can be partially load bearing).

Next, look at which way the floorboards are running. A load-bearing wall will be at a right angle to the joists (because it is supporting them) and the floorboards on top of the joists will be perpendicular to those, so if the floorboards run in the same direction as the wall, it is likely that the wall is load bearing. But to be really sure, you would need to lift a floorboard, as new floorboards may have been laid on the original.

Once you have identified which walls are structural, obtain a drawing of the house and colour in those walls to show which walls you ideally don't want to take out. Working within

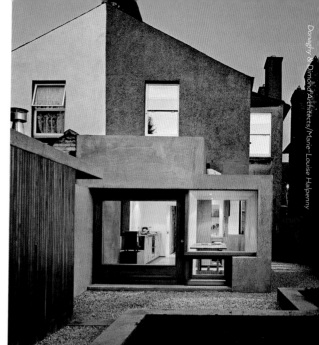

structural walls will keep costs down, but if you find that the house would work much better if you broke through a structural wall (and put in the necessary supplementary structure), then the couple of thousand euro it will cost could be well worth it.

You may not be able to take out the whole wall; you will need to leave a nib to support the new steel structure that will take on the load-bearing task. Get a structural engineer to inspect the wall and recommend the amount of steel support needed. They will be able to supply a certificate to say that it complies with building regulations.

Another obstruction to opening up a space is an old fireplace. If you are taking it out, it is worth taking it out all the way up the house to free up space in upstairs bedrooms and in the attic. If removing the fireplace frees up the whole plan (and part of the section), it is well worth doing.

EXTENDING UPSTAIRS

The cheapest way of putting a second floor on an extension is when you are building the extension in the first place. If you are building a single-storey extension and imagine that you may need more space above at a later date, try to do it now. That way you will only have to put the roof on once. If you have to strip off the roof in a few years' time, you lose the price you paid for it the first time around.

MATERIALS

A lot of people, especially in older houses, try to match the extension to the existing house. It is impossible to do this successfully with a brick that looks like the original or windows that are just a version of what went before, for instance. The golden rule is that if you are going to use the same materials, they have to be exactly the same, and the construction methods – using the same type of mortar, for instance – must tie in so closely that the two parts feel as if they were conceived at the same time. If you try to do a mish-mash of the two parts, it never really works.

For a lot of extensions, then, unless you can marry the two structures perfectly, it is a good idea to go for a complete contrast – in all sorts of properties, especially older ones but also 1960s and 70s houses, farmhouses and so on – so that people can read what's old and what's new.

A really good way to do this is to change the material. If the existing building is in stone, then consider brick; if the main building is in brick, then use render or another contrasting material. Even conservation bodies whose remit is to preserve old buildings agree that being able to read the old and the new is the best way to add an extension.

When building an extension, be honest with the materials. A big trend in the boom was to add cladding, with stone or timber pasted on like wallpaper, which looks (and is) fake and weathers badly. Instead, use bricks, blockwork with render or actual local stone.

box architecture/Paul Tierney

When there are rooflights, I love it when they run along the central ridge of the roof.

FLAT ROOF

While people tend to be frightened of flat roofs on extensions, architects have been using them for years. They make sense because they are less likely than a pitched roof to block light from a first-floor window on the main house that overlooks the extension, and in a single-storey extension they allow for a higher ceiling overall.

Yet almost as part of the brief, people start off by saying, 'We won't be having a flat roof.' The reason why people are nervous about flat roofs is that those built in the middle of the 20th century onwards were often poorly insulated and were prone to leaks. Technology has moved on and flat roofs are now constructed in a different way to allow the roof to breathe. The modern insulation means that there are no problems with condensation like there were in the past, they don't leak and the timbers don't rot. As a sign of confidence, they often come with 10-, 20-, 30- and even 40-year guarantees. If you think about it, schools, hospitals, airports and so on have flat roofs that work perfectly well.

THE ROOF

PITCHED ROOF

If you opt for a pitched roof, carefully consider where to put the collar or tie beam. These pieces of timber tie the roof together inside (running from one side to another) and should be as high as possible. There is nothing nicer than seeing the whole height of a roof from within, giving space and light. This may mean using extra steel support in the roof or being cleverer with the construction, and it may cost more, but the extra ceiling height gained will be worth it.

Aughey O'Flaherty Architects/Marie-Louise Halpenny

Amanda Bone Architects/Ros Kavanagh

MONO-PITCHED ROOF

A mono-pitched roof, with one wall higher than the other, gives more flexibility in the way the extension joins the house and so can be cheaper. It also means you don't have to tie two sides of the roof together, as you do with a standard pitched roof.

It is an economic way to get a lovely high ceiling. It does mean that you will have one tall wall, so you need to consider what this faces onto and how it can be broken up with windows.

LOW-PITCHED ROOF

If someone really doesn't want a flat roof, a low-pitched roof can be a good alternative. Many recent examples across Ireland have used copper, lead or zinc as a covering. It can have a pavilion feel to it that looks good from the garden.

As with a flat roof, a low-pitched roof doesn't detract from the existing house by obstructing light to a first-floor window.

Aughey O'Flaherty Architects/Marie-Louise Halpenny

Donaghy & Dimond Architects/Ros Kavanagh

MAKING AN EXTENSION WORK

When building an extension, people always think of having a great big kitchen, living room, playroom or home office, but it can also be used to solve problems. Houses need storage space, a utility area and a boiler room, and an extension can accommodate these. Don't put them at the bottom of your wish list – if they are done right, they will make the whole house work better. Don't just be seduced by the kitchen – factor in ordinary things too.

A well-designed extension can also bring light into formerly dark parts of a home. Have a good look at dark spaces in the house and see if the extension could bring light to these (see Chapter 2 on light and volumes).

EXTENDING INTO THE ATTIC

If you are looking for some extra space for a bedroom, a study, a home office or even a second living space as a refuge for teenagers, the answer may be above your head in an unused attic. There is something about loft or attic spaces that can have a dramatically different feel to the rest of the house – it's something to do with being able to feel the shape of the roof or how far away it can be from the rest of the house that can make it feel special.

Most of us use the attic for storage and most attics are packed to the gills, but probably with stuff we don't need and could be thrown out. Do a proper cull and you will find that the space that remains at the edge of an attic conversion is plenty for your needs.

You need to ensure that you have enough ceiling height. The biggest mistake people make when converting their attic is not having a high enough ceiling in the roof. This not only restricts living space, but when selling the house, what they thought was a bedroom can only be called a store room. It's all to do with ventilation – the space needs to be high enough for air to circulate.

As a general rule of thumb, half of your floor area in the new room must have a ceiling height of 2.4 metres (8 feet). A large dormer window in the right place may really help your calculations and turn it into a proper room.

Your stairs up to the space also need to have the correct dimensions. Again, this could be a barrier to selling your home in the future. I see so many attic conversions with really narrow or steep stairs up to it – you shouldn't put in stairs that don't comply with the building regulations. I would advise a maximum step height of 210mm and a minimum depth of a step of 220mm – this is steep, but it complies. Also check the regulations for where you can introduce twists and turns in your stairs. It's also worth looking at where the stairs are located. There is no point losing a room downstairs to accommodate them or to have them arrive in a location upstairs that you are potentially banging your head on or that it messes up the room completely by dividing it up too much.

The light and views from an attic room can be fantastic, as you are up in the treetops! You can put a rooflight to the rear of your house without planning permission, but any rooflights that are to the side or front or any dormer window structures will require planning permission. As mentioned before, a tall enough dormer window may solve your ceiling height problems, but it can have a dramatic impact on the exterior of the house, especially if your house is in the middle of a terrace or is one half of a semi-detached. Your choice of material is crucial so as not to jar with the existing roofscape – try to choose materials and colours that will blend in with the existing slates or tiles.

Always have an engineer look at your floor structure to ensure it is strong enough. What may be okay to hold the weight of a couple of suitcases may not hold you and your bed. Older houses have great attic spaces but nearly always need to have their floor strengthened. The impact of this is that the

Peter Legge Associates

The attic space will always be a little more awkward to lay out than a room in the rest of the house on account of the sloping walls. It is really worth placing all the furniture, especially beds, on a drawing, bearing in mind the ceiling height in that location to ensure no banging of heads!

One final thing to remember is that if your house is already two storeys high, then your conversion now makes your house three storeys, which means that you will need to comply with fire regulations. In theory it is possible to jump or be rescued from a first-floor window in case of a fire, but not from a third-floor attic room, so you will need to ensure that you have an escape route from the third floor that is protected from a fire breaking out in another room. You can achieve this by putting fire doors onto all rooms that open out onto the hall stairs and landing. These doors will need self-closing hinges in case you forget to keep them shut. These are all easy to retro fit into an existing house, but you will need to set aside some money in your budget for it.

new timbers that are required to ensure that the floor is strong enough may be much taller than the existing ones, which could impact your floor to ceiling dimensions. It is worth having all of these calculations done before you embark on the project.

You will lose storage space when you convert the attic, but you would be surprised at how much leftover space there is. Try to use the edges of the room, where the ceiling is low, to introduce storage. This area can be great for low wardrobes, built-in drawers or a simple low door that allows storage in this space. If the space is long and narrow, you can divide up a section dedicated to storage with its own door. This space doesn't need to be finished off to the same standard as the rest of the conversion, so it may even keep the budget a little lower.

Sterrin O'Shea Architects

CHAPTER 7

HOLDING COURT

The use of courtyards in architecture has been around for a very long time. In warmer, southern climates they were, and are, used to cool buildings by leaving windows and doors open onto this shadowed, private space (a fountain, spraying water and negative ions, would add beautifully to the cooling effect). In Ireland and the UK, courtyards helped to make a fortress of the building, with the inward core protected during battles, as well as offering shelter from prevailing winds and other harsh weather and keeping livestock in place.

instance where a barn becomes a courtyard wall. I love that about Irish rural design – how buildings are used to form courtyards, perhaps between a cow and a pig barn to keep livestock in.

These enclosed spaces could also be used to create walled gardens. Walled vegetable gardens on large country estates are lovely sheltered spaces that are still used and appreciated today. In houses that are open to the public, this is often where tea rooms are placed so that people can sit outside.

In Ireland they have recently tended to be confined to apartment blocks, yet they abound on a smaller scale in traditional Irish architecture. Our farmsteads have historically created courtyards among buildings in a well-thought-out way, for

Dermot Bannon Architects

For all their practicality, courtyards are also romantic. People love the idea of them in Florentine palazzos, Tuscan villas, French chateaux and amid clusters of farm buildings, not to mention the Louvre in Paris. I absolutely love courtyards. They offer an outside but private realm completely under the control of the inhabitants of a house.

GREET AND MEET

In a good design, people will be encouraged to traverse the courtyard and interact on it. Designs should keep in mind that the courtyard should be a meeting place, so it helps if there are activities on two sides of the courtyard (in fact, the courtyard could just have two sides): for instance, bedrooms along one part and a kitchen or living room on the other. This encourages the use of the courtyard as a circulation route, just as they were in monasteries, where they served as the public realm.

This shows how activities around the courtyard work really well. When sitting on one side of the courtyard looking across, it is pleasant to be able to see beyond the wall, through glass into activity beyond.

LARGE COURTYARDS

Farmers in Ireland understood how buildings formed enclosures to control the environment and provide shelter and protection, and there is an amazing array of courtyards in our countryside enclosed by old, vernacular buildings. As they added new buildings into the smallholding, people would place them at right angles to each other to create sheltered spots. This is worth remembering today when extending a house – if you add the new part at a right angle, you will create a sheltered area, making at least two sides of a courtyard.

Find out where the prevailing wind comes from and which part traps the sun so that you can create a pleasant area to sit out in; this provision of shelter is where a courtyard comes into its own. When doing this, remember the rule about having different, but linked, activities in each leg, such as a kitchen, living and/or dining area along one side and bedrooms on the other.

If you have, or are constructing, outbuildings, consider how these can form another edge to your courtyard or create a new one. Hedges, trees and shrubs can also be used to create a virtual third wall to a courtyard to add to the sense of enclosure. There can be gaps in them to frame views.

box architecture/Paul Tierney

MEDIUM, LINEAR COURTYARDS

....

If you have a long, narrow back garden and want to build up against boundaries, then you can create a courtyard by extending along the side and across the rear of the site, using the buildings to form the edges of a courtyard in the middle. This will create a perfect outdoor space on such a site, offering a breathing space and bringing natural light into a linear building.

When creating this, be aware of the 6 metre rule: in a standard single-storey structure, the building will create a shadow 6 metres long (this works in multiples, so at two storeys the shadow will be pushed to 12 metres and so on), so you'll need an outdoor space that goes beyond this if you want to get sun. However, you can still create a courtyard that is shorter than this, as the light and ventilation are welcome too.

Dermot Bannon Architects

SMALL COURTYARDS

Architects have recently made inventive use of tiny courtyards (some less than a metre wide) as a great way of bringing light, life and ventilation into terraced houses (and others) that are being extended. Adding onto houses can create a land-locked central room that becomes a dark space. Having a tiny courtyard is a way of adding a light well that brightens up all the rooms in a house. For instance, you can extend a hallway, creating a courtyard beside it, and put the kitchen beyond it: the courtyard then brings light into the extension and the room(s) beside it in the existing house. It can also be a way of bringing ventilation into a bathroom on the ground floor.

However small it is, it is worth bringing life into a courtyard through planting, by having tables and chairs in it or a place to pass through. This is preferable to it being a sterile space with just, say, gravel. It can be a little lung in the middle of the house.

Rooms to Improve

CHAPTER 8

KITCHENS

Donaghy & Dimond Architects/Luke White

Donal Colfer/Alice Clancy

The kitchen is the heart and soul of every home. People gather here and it is usually the most heavily used room in the house, so it needs to be planned well.

THE CASE FOR OPEN PLAN

People often say they know what they want, but in reality it can be a case of wanting what they know. They need a paradigm shift. They think that because they have grown up with something, it works for them.

I see the same problems over and over again because lots of people live in houses designed by developers or built from a plan in a bungalow book. There is often not enough natural light and the flow through the house can be poor. This is because many homes are throwbacks to Victorian houses, with a living room at the front, a dining room in the middle and the kitchen at the back. All these small rooms that don't connect well make it feel very segregated. Connecting a living and dining space back to the kitchen makes a house so much easier to live in.

When my clients outline their problems, often the solution is an open-plan family space – although that can take some persuasion. I would never

Dermot Bannon Architects/
Aidee Cavanagh

Donaghy & Dimond Architects/Philip Lauterbach

persuade a client to do something they really didn't want to do, but they will often answer conundrums for themselves, for instance by saying they can't see their kids in another room or that it is really dark in their kitchen.

Sometimes holiday homes can be a revelation and give an indication of what open-plan living is like. People who live in huge houses with segregated rooms can find that they really enjoy three weeks with their family in a caravan.

The pluses of open plan far outweigh the minuses and lots of issues can be resolved. For instance, some people say that they don't like the smell of cooking, but a good extractor solves that. I love when clients who have switched to an open-plan kitchen/dining area contact me after a year and say, 'It has transformed how we live.'

MAKING OPEN PLAN WORK

The open-plan area needs to be a family space that allows for social interaction, so you do need to set up rules. For instance, if somebody wants to watch sports or a soap by themselves, they probably need a separate den; there is no reason why the television should be in the open-plan space.

When considering a design, think about your future needs. An open-plan space is great for keeping an eye on very young children, but what about when they are seven? And teenagers? And how will the house work when it becomes an 'empty nest'? Talk to friends and family about their experiences of these milestones. Solutions

Steve Larkin Architects/Alice Clancy

If you inherit a north-facing kitchen and are in there nearly 90 per cent of the time, then it might be worth considering moving it or opening up whatever room is blocking light. If you are spending time there, then it needs to be in the right location.

Amanda Bone Architects/Ros Kavanagh

could be having a playroom or office beside the kitchen. Sliding glazed screens can be another answer, which close off spaces when need be without losing natural light.

THE SUNNY SIDE

A kitchen should be in the south or east of a home. South is ideal, for all-day sun. To form a brief, I ask clients to describe their week. Most families have routines – there might be a day in the week when somebody is at home, and often families get together at the weekend. If, for instance, clients say that they are in the kitchen most mornings, preparing food, and then out all afternoon and return at 5pm, then the kitchen should face east (for morning sun) and a dining space to the west.

Steerin O'Shea Architects

CONNECTING WITH NATURE

Attaching the garden to a well-used kitchen and dining area makes sense – for eating outside, throwing open the doors on warm days, keeping an eye on children playing outside, ease of access to a compost bin and for making the most of any vegetables and herbs you grow. In my house we have a patio beside the kitchen where we have planted herbs.

Eating outside is a new thing for us. My dad wouldn't have a barbecue; he insisted on cooking inside and then eating outside quickly. He associated cooking outside with working on the farm. The generations in Ireland who worked outside liked to come into the kitchen, away from the sun, but now many of us sit in offices all day long and we need a connection to nature.

YOUR IDEAL KITCHEN

Think about what works for you in your current kitchen. What are your likes and dislikes? There are often eccentricities about a kitchen that people grow to like even if they are not there by design. They are worth keeping: I do find that people often want to get rid of everything needlessly.

BASICS AND LAYOUTS

The work triangle is an efficient way to lay out a kitchen because it allows for ease of movement and use. The triangle involves three main activity areas: fridge, cooking and the sink. It should be easy to move between the three without encountering chairs, a table or an island unit, and they should be fairly close together. Each area should be beside a surface you can put things on, even temporarily. The key question, though, is how you use your kitchen. After discussing it with your architect, if you feel a rigid triangle will not work for you, then that is fine.

Donaghy & Dimond Architects

L-SHAPED

This kitchen has units along two adjacent walls and allows for the perfect work triangle. Work surfaces between each element in the triangle allow for optimum use of the kitchen. This layout does create a corner, but 'magic corner' units that swing right out make good use of this space.

U-SHAPED

This kitchen uses three walls and has the potential for the most storage and work space. A disadvantage is that it can dominate a room, feel enclosed and restrict the size of windows. If it is in a large space, avoid too much travelling between the elements in the work triangle by placing them at the base of the U. You can zone the spaces by having, for instance, one whole wall for tall units,

double ovens and the fridge. You need a minimum 1.4 metre width of space to walk in in the middle; more than 2.4 metres is too much, as it creates a lost, wasted space that is not big enough to put a table in. Magic corner units work well in this type of kitchen too.

LINEAR

This involves one long run of units and is
good for tight spaces or for placing in a dining
room to allow for a table with room around it.
It does dispense with the triangle (although a
dining table can become something of a third
element), but all the walking up and down
can be worth it if it means the room is more
efficient.

Make sure you leave enough space between
the hob and sink, and make sure the
countertop is long and deep enough for
kettles, toasters and so on (these normally get
shoved into a corner, which you won't have
here). A 900mm deep countertop is ideal
(with pull-out drawers so items don't get lost
at the back of cupboards), as you can put
things at the back of it and still have enough
counter space to work on in front of them.
A small shelf at the back of the counter at a
higher level can also be a good idea.

PENINSULAR

This kitchen runs along one wall and has a
separate work surface jutting from another
wall, usually parallel to the main units. This
allows for flexibility – the main work space can
be positioned to overlook, say, the main dining
space or a good view. On the downside, it can
feel a bit enclosed. Similar to this is a linear
kitchen with an island unit.

ISLAND

An island is a great working space and also connects to the rest of the room by providing a gathering space to put chairs around. It makes cooking very social by bringing people together. If two or more people regularly cook together in your kitchen, then an island unit will give you each your own space to move about in.

Islands do take up a lot of space and there are lots of badly designed ones without enough space around them. Try to get at least 1 metre of space beyond the island to fit in chairs and to allow people to pass.

The island needs to be between 900mm and 1.2 metres deep. Ours is 650mm deep and it just doesn't work: when anyone's baking, flour ends up on the floor and a fruit bowl takes up nearly all of it.

The optimum length is 1.8 metres to 2.4 metres; anything bigger can be too big. I did once make one that was 3 metres long, but after this it starts to get too big to move around. At 1.8 metres you can get a sink or hob into it and still have space on each side of it.

If you are linking an island with a linear kitchen, you will achieve a work triangle by putting a sink or hob into the island unit.

You should have an optimum 1.4 metres of space between the units and the island. Kitchen manufacturers say 1.2 metres will suffice, but that doesn't allow enough room for two people to work back to back. It also gives enough clearance to stop doors crashing into each other.

MY WISH LIST

▶ A tall unit for a fridge/freezer – the ideal would be to have separate, tall larder fridges and freezers

▶ A tall unit to integrate the oven at eye level with storage above and below

▶ A kitchen with a pantry unit 600mm wide full of food and heavy equipment such as a standalone mixer

▶ Three tall units together

▶ Try to steer clear of deep cupboards and use pull-out drawers so that everything doesn't get stuck at the back

▶ A dishwasher

▶ A good bin that allows you to recycle at source

Dermot Bannon Architects/Enda Cavanagh

KITCHEN STYLES
FOR MODERN LIFE

·····································

We have a fondness for country-style kitchens. I like to interpret country kitchens in a contemporary way while making contemporary kitchens warm and simple: this way, neither of them will date.

A kitchen should be contemporary: it's a piece of furniture that needs to become a machine and work really well and effortlessly. People have fixed ideas about the type of kitchen they want. While I don't want to impose my views on them, I do encourage people to steer clear of pastiche (imitating the past).

COUNTRY

I get clients to cut out images from magazines and books, and if they keep coming back to country farmhouse kitchens, I try to understand what they like about it. Sometimes it is the ornateness: people like stuck-on bits because they think it looks expensive. To create a contemporary version of this, introduce 'extras' via details such as a contrasting worktop.

Another attraction of country kitchens is that people like their unfitted quality. With modern services it is very difficult to have an unfitted kitchen, and I feel that we have become accustomed to a marketing view of what a country kitchen is: a Laura Ashley version of life. In reality, an old Irish kitchen had three pieces of furniture and a table in the middle.

You can create an unfitted, country feel in a long, linear kitchen by introducing verticality and contrasting materials, such as adding walnut legs to a pale timber kitchen or by expressing the frame in a different material to give it another level of detail. To keep the palette clean, spray-paint the doors while keeping the frame in solid wood or plywood to add warmth. Another option would be to introduce a veneer or solid timber doors to give it that warmth in a flat, contemporary way.

Peter Legge Associates

CONTEMPORARY

porary kitchens are my favourite
they work well in open-plan spaces,
ed to be quiet and blend into the
love it when everything is hidden
no handles. I can labour for hours
ing to line up. With all the different
n behind the ordered façade, you

need to treat it like a jigsaw puzzle or Rubik's
Cube. Get all of the shapes flattened onto a
drawing: dishwashers, fridge/freezer and so on –
and move them around until it all makes sense
and a rhythm and structure is set up. When the
two work well together, it becomes a really good
piece of design.

MATERIALS

To keep kitchen costs down, use standard off-the-shelf carcasses and spend your money on anything you touch and feel. The things you interact with – worktops, doors, handles, taps – should be the best quality you can afford.

DOORS

Solid wood can look great if it is designed well. If you have a frame and panel, it risks looking overly fussy. A flat timber veneer door with a hardwood edge can be more forgiving and can look elegant, while MDF veneered with timber and a hardwood lipping around it can give a lovely warmth.

One of my favourite materials is plywood made of layers of veneers laid in alternate directions, giving it a lovely striped edge.

Laminated doors – in Formica or vinyl, for instance – give a really cool, sleek, contemporary look. The very flat, even finish was made popular with high-gloss kitchens over the last few years, and although I like them, my favourite is a flat, matt finish.

Spray-painted doors are a fantastic way to introduce colour into a kitchen and create a strong element in the room. You can also play around with colours and materials. If you have an island unit and a bank of units behind, you can play with contrast. In one project I used pale grey on the main units and a darker grey on the island. This can help break down the scale of a kitchen and make it feel freer – more like a piece of furniture than a fitted kitchen.

DOOR HANDLES

When choosing door handles, don't just look at them in the showroom – place them on a number of doors. Also make sure they feel comfortable in your hand. When placing them in your kitchen, be aware of the overall pattern. Express them in cool stainless steel and chrome. An alternative that I love is to have no handles at all.

INSTALLING DOORS

Consider how the doors will be hinged. For instance, if you have a hob next to a wall unit you don't want the door to open into your face, as it will be difficult to get something, such as a spice, from the cupboard while you're cooking. Doors should also be hung so that they don't hit or cover other items of furniture when they are open. It's worth considering having adjoining doors opening away from each other so that you can grab the handles in the middle, open both doors together and see what's in the entire space all at once. Ideally, cupboards that contain frequently used items should be between eye and knee height and shouldn't be more than 60cm deep. To save your back, you can have pull-out cupboards so that the items come out to meet you. With a pull-out larder you can peer in from both sides. This will save you from buying your 20th tin of plum tomatoes, as you can see exactly what you have in your cupboards.

WORKTOPS

Spend as much as you can afford on a worktop because it gets a lot of wear and tear and is prone to damage. Also, because it is horizontal, you are looking at it often and close up. The ideal kitchen worktop is non-porous, doesn't stain or scratch and requires very little maintenance and cleaning.

Ideally a working surface should be 5–10cm lower than the height of your flexed elbow. Think about having a small shelf running along the back of the surface to put items such as washing-up liquid and cooking oil on – you can also park items up here when you clean the surface. Some materials, such as metal and Corian, can be moulded to form this as an integral part of the worktop.

If you are changing a worktop in an existing kitchen and have a built-in hob and sink, you'll need to disconnect the plumbing, gas and electricity. The worktop may be screwed down or glued. If it's glued you'll probably have to break the old worktop to remove it.

STONE

My favourite material is natural stone, such as granite, slate, marble and limestone. Some stone, such as pale marble, may need to be sealed because it picks up stains, such as a ring from a glass of red wine left on it. But white marble can really brighten up a space. Many types of slate are porous too, but slate with a high silica content is suitable and provides a cool, matt surface. Granite comes in many colours, from plain black to granite with sparkling flecks. Black granite has been a stalwart because it creates a cool, calm backdrop in kitchens, which tend to have a lot going on in them.

Dermot Bannon Architects/Ros Kavanagh

Dermot Bannon Architects/Ros Kavanagh

QUARTZ AND CORIAN

My second favourites are quartz or Corian. Quartz is reconstituted concrete with stone and shells mixed to a beautiful finish. It comes in an amazing range of colours.

Corian is made of reconstituted, recycled plastic (acrylic polymer and alumina trihydrate). The beauty of Corian is that it is versatile and can be moulded into sinks, shapes and so on, providing an incredible and uniform surface.

TIMBER

I have timber in my own house, which I love for its warmth, but areas around sinks or areas that take abuse do need to be taken care of and oiled. If I was doing my kitchen again, I would opt for quartz or granite near the sink.

Oil your wooden worktop as much as you can when you first get it, and regularly after that. This keeps it supple and smooth and helps it to withstand heat, scratching and moisture. Hardwoods, such as oak and iroko, are more resistant to heat and stains.

The beauty of wood is that it ages well – it can look stunning even after years of use. Chefs love timber because it has bounce and is naturally hygienic. If you put a knife on granite or quartz it can blunt, and plates dropped on it are more likely to smash.

Amanda Bone Architects/Ros Kavanagh

Sterrin O'Shea Architects

If you are using timber anywhere in the kitchen, try to tie it in with the joinery in the house or else create a strong contrast, such as using dark teak or walnut against oak.

The gap between a sink and wooden worktop needs to be sealed well. Wood moves, so the seal between a wooden worktop and the sink may eventually break, bringing the surface into contact with water, which can eventually rot wood. (The same problem occurs where tiling meets an element such as a wall or hob. The grouting recess can be susceptible to damage and wear.)

LAMINATE

Formed laminate worktops come in really bright colours, so you can be playful with them. I hate fake timber or marble though, which every apartment in Dublin seemed to have during the boom. Use block colours such as black, grey, orange or red. If it is a laminate on a chipboard backing, don't let water into any cracks, as this will rot the interior. It's also not a good surface for cutting food on, as it scratches.

TILES

While tiling looks good on floors and walls, as a work surface it comes under close scrutiny and you are able to see every flaw. The tiles themselves may be hard-wearing, but the grout can stain if it is damaged and gets wet.

METAL

Stainless steel is used in many professional kitchens because it's heat resistant, hard-wearing, hygienic and non-corrosive. However, it can scratch easily, although brushed stainless steel is more hard-wearing and doesn't show up scratches as much as the polished variety. It can also be a noisy surface to work on.

Copper is another metal used for worktops and was common in old bars.

GLASS

Glass, either clear or frosted, is an exciting material to use as a worktop. Because it is transparent you do have to have a backing, such as white MDF (medium density fibreboard).

ERGONOMICS

There are standard sizes for kitchens and unit heights, but you can adapt them to your needs. A well-designed, bespoke kitchen won't make you strain your back by bending at an awkward level (your back should ideally be straight or slightly curved) or make you do repetitive tasks in one position.

Standard worktop heights range between 85cm and 95cm, but ideally the worktop should be around 5–10cm below the height of your flexed elbow. You can either have units made to suit you or adjust levels by adapting the plinths beneath the units.

Some kitchen designers feel that beyond a certain age it will be difficult to bend down to get dishes in and out of a dishwasher at ground level or an oven near the ground (ideally it should be between eye and waist level). But then, my 80-year-old granny easily bent down to get a chicken from her Aga. Everyone is different.

▶ What are your priorities?

▶ What do you use the kitchen for?

▶ Do you like to cook?

▶ What do you cook?

▶ Do you make a lot of pastries? If so, then you need a good granite surface as opposed to a wooden countertop.

▶ How often do you cook?

▶ Do you cook a breakfast every day?

▶ Do you cook a lunch every day?

▶ Do you cook for kids?

▶ How much space do you need? A working professional might just use a microwave, while others might have extended family over a lot.

▶ What kind of storage do you need? Do you buy food daily or once a week?

▶ How many appliances do you want on show? For example, is there a big espresso machine that will take pride of place?

▶ Do you cook a lot of Chinese food, putting lots of oil and ingredients into a hot wok? If so, you need really good extraction.

THE IRISH LOVE AFFAIR WITH THE TABLE

Irish people love to hang out in the kitchen and the table is very much at the root of it. In my family we had a kitchen table and a good dining table that was used only twice a year. Family discussions were always around the kitchen table, even though it was a really tight space. If you wanted to get to the dishwasher, five people had to move. There'd be bits of food left over on the table at home, which we would pick at for hours – food puts people at ease.

You get more gossip at a table than in living room chairs. Even in *Downton Abbey*, all the good chats happen around the table. People like having a table in front of them; it's a security thing. Half of our body is covered and we can kick off our shoes and we love the comfort of resting our elbows on it.

The farmhouse table, with everything going on around it, is embedded in the Irish psyche. Because of that, it is something you really need to be mindful of in kitchen design: in a big open-plan space, the table needs to be very much part of the cooking area.

Peter Legge Associates

CHAPTER 9

LIVING ROOMS

'No homogenous room, of homogenous height, can serve a group of people well. To give a group a chance to be together, a room must also give them a chance to be alone in ones and twos.'
– *A Pattern Language*

WHAT'S IN A NAME?

....

The sheer number of names this room has – living, lounge, sitting, front, drawing – underlines just how much activity (or inactivity) it potentially needs to accommodate. Those in huge houses could have a room to suit each activity – hence the drawing room, which people could withdraw into or the 16th-century aristocrat could hide in,

Ailtir(eacht)

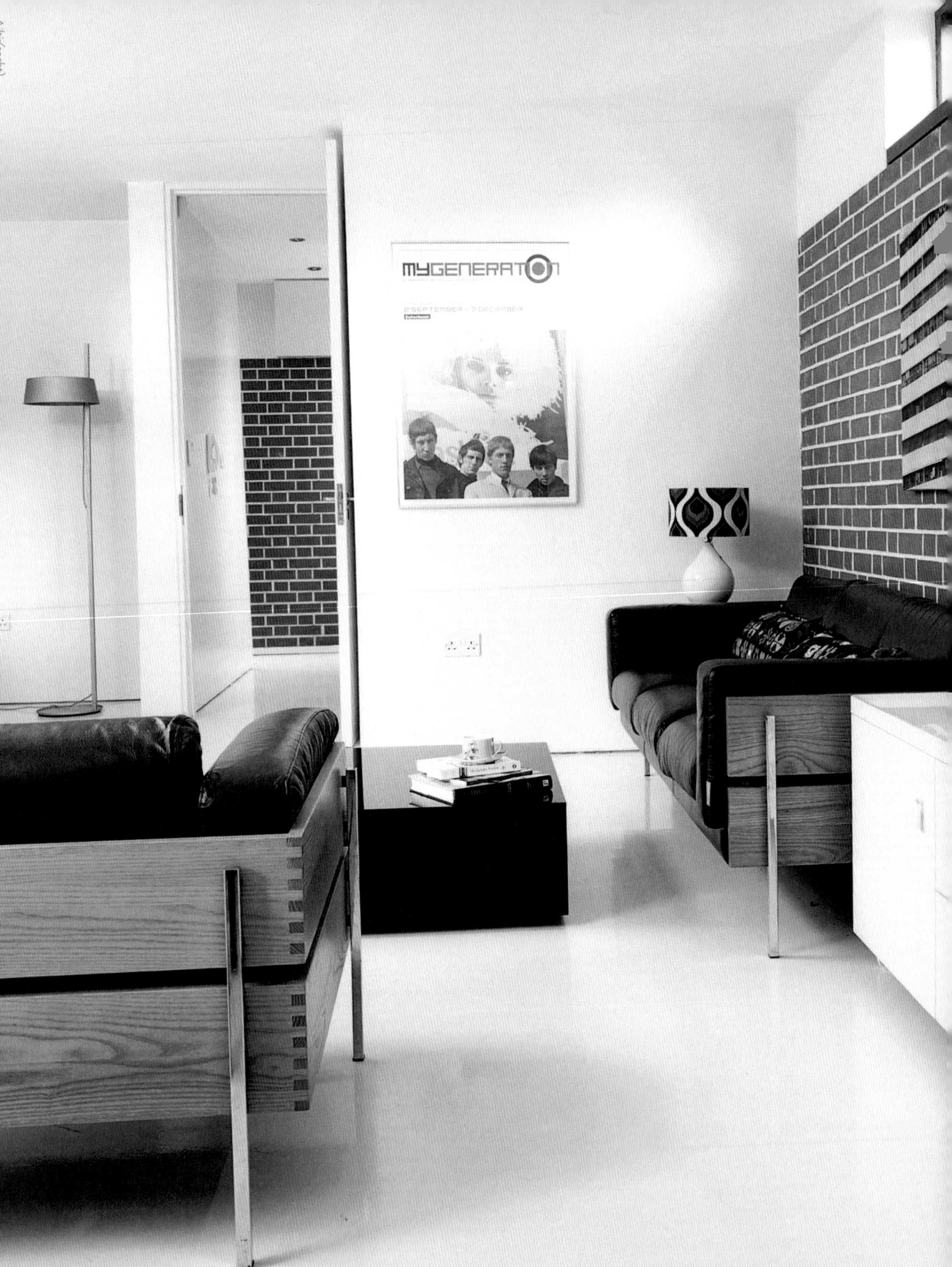

away from the more public quarters of the manor, to a gathering place for the ruling classes before or after dinner, to just a separate room to usher any guests into. This latter use manifested as the parlour in Irish houses: the good room into which visitors were shown.

As many Irish families will recall, priests and other visitors were ushered into this 'good room' – or parlour – at the front of the house. Such visiting rites involved literally putting up a front: signs of poverty and disharmony were hidden from view, along with a clatter of children for the duration of a social call. Being at the front of the homestead, this good room was also a sales pitch for passers-by, who were encouraged to think its inhabitants were quite affluent.

From the 1960s onwards, when people became increasingly well off and relaxed and other rooms improved, visitors began to be brought into those areas of the home, or the kitchen. Since then, greater parts of our homes have opened up to people. But many people are still designing houses in the old style of keeping a 'good room'. While it can work for some lifestyles, it needs to be a considered decision.

It is not only the guests who are now spreading through the house – the living spaces are too as other rooms double up. And with all that is done in living spaces – listening to music, reading, doing crosswords, knitting, chatting, playing games, entertaining and watching television – it helps if other parts of the home can take on some of those roles if possible to relieve the pressure on the one space. For example, people may gather to chat in the kitchen, or even watch TV there.

PARTY OR APART

There is a choice: having a living room as part of an open-plan space, perhaps as part of a kitchen and/or dining area; having it connected to the rest of the house in some way (through double doors, for instance); or having it as a completely separate space. Wherever it is, it needs to be functional and comfortable, and capable of being busy and calm.

It also needs to be flexible. Sometimes it will need to accommodate large groups, such as a book club or families and friends, while at other times smaller groups will use it. Or sometimes there might even be groups of smaller groups, such as three people chatting, two listening to music, two playing a game and so on.

One of my clients was a woman with 20 children and grandchildren who had separated from her husband. She lived alone but regularly had family to visit, so I had to design a room that catered for all her grandchildren but also suited her when she was alone in the evenings. I used a wood-burning stove to divide the space loosely when family was visiting and to create a cosy setting for when they were not, with lighting that could be turned off in the background so that the room size 'shrank'.

If I design a big house, I still suggest a break-out space – not everyone wants to watch a match or box sets on the telly. The separate space doesn't need to have the formality that a former sitting room typically had, but with all the activity happening elsewhere in a home, a living room can even turn into a quiet room for finding some solitude.

In my house, a two-up, two-down with an extension, we have an open-plan kitchen/living/ dining space where the children play (there are usually toys on the floor), where we sometimes watch DVDs and where friends gather round the dining table and on the couch. I kept the really small room at the front of the house as a place to read in, watch TV or movies as a family, and to sit round the fire. I see it as an escape from the main house. We use it as an evening room and I love it. When you're in there, you're in unwind mode. There are no pots to wash, dinners to cook, no homework or toys to clear up. We don't even bring visitors in there – the open-plan space is for them, which is opposite to how it was in the past. It is like the family snug.

PLANNING THE FOCUS OF YOUR ROOM

A living room can be a complicated room to plan and you need to decide early on what the focus will be. I see this as being a choice, or relationship, between the TV, the fire and the view. The three of them can fight with each other, so it is a challenge.

It can be constricting because sometimes when we are designing we like to open up one wall to a view. Another conundrum in our office is trying to get a wall long enough to have both the fire and TV on it. That is not to say, though, that you can't interact with two of the three main focus areas at a time (for instance, the view and the fire).

TELEVISION

I'm not a big fan of having the TV as the focus of a room and I definitely don't want it to dominate so much that it is the first thing you see when you walk into a living room. Alternatives are to try to design it so that the TV drifts into the background of the room or have a white wall that you can project programmes onto. For the rest of the time you could keep most of this equipment hidden, perhaps in a cupboard or behind a sofa.

FIRE

You can't underestimate the importance of a fire. They never went out of favour in Ireland, and even in the 1970s, when the world seemed to be moving away from them, you would still see open fires in Ireland. Then there is the perennial range in the kitchen: a cosy heart of the home and something to warm your backside against.

It's no wonder humans have such an affinity with it. Fire is an element, along with water, air and earth, and a core part of existence and nature. It is so relaxing, even for children. When I sit in front of ours with my two-year-old son he can be quiet for minutes, just staring into the flames.

A fire needs to form part of a circle, with seating around it – a welcome place for family and friends to gather. And yet, while a fire anchors a sitting room, it has recently become more about the style and positioning of it. Fires are now seen as a luxury item and the focus has increasingly become about the surround rather than the fire itself. People obsess over symmetry too, concentrating on it 'looking right' rather than how it feels, which is a shame.

Donaghy & Dimond Architects/Ros Kavanagh

Robert Bourke Architects/Alice Clancy

THE VIEW

Everybody loves to sit by a window, so position a seat here or even design in a window seat. Bay windows make a lovely setting for a built-in seat or a carefully chosen piece of furniture.

It is nice to look out of a window from other parts of the room when seated, so lower the sill if possible. Mirrors are a great way of reflecting and bouncing natural light around and can even reflect the view out if they are positioned at an angle to the window.

Window treatments can also be used to create certain effects. Heavy curtains in a cold house make a room warmer, while in a dark, busy space, a light roller blind can help make a room feel bigger, brighter and calmer.

Dermot Bannon Architects

FURNITURE LAYOUT

A lot of seating areas are sterile and seem as if they have been set up for a photograph. How the layout feels (rather than looks) is hugely important: a living space needs to gather life around it, to concentrate and liberate energy.

Try to arrange the space so that people can organise themselves in a circle. People like to sit at an angle to each other, not side by side, so single chairs or small sofas are worth considering – or, conversely, a huge sofa. Just not a couch that forces people to sit primly beside each other.

Chairs will only remain in a spot if the space holds them and defines the area. Chairs, sofas and cushions can be in a loose arrangement so that people feel they can move them around in

Aughey O'Flaherty Architects/Grand Designs

Dermot Bannon Architects

an informal manner. They can be placed closer together and in a circle for chats, then moved to face the fire or TV straight on when you're screen- or flame-gazing.

Use flexible items, such as bean bags and stools, which can even be moved to different rooms when they are needed, or stacked away.

CIRCULATION

Because the living room has to function on so many different levels, it can be complicated to design (although in reality, living spaces tend to evolve rather than be created in one go).

If you want to get technical, prescriptive and organised, you could follow the interior designers' method of creating a plan of the room on graph paper (or computer) and adding cut-outs of scaled-down pieces of furniture and permanent fixtures. You can go into detail, such as showing where drawers, doors and windows open. Then either rearrange everything to see how it would work, or when buying new furniture, get the dimensions and see how it would fit into the space before you buy. Remember that a sofa that looks small in a showroom may look vast in your house. But even before you get to its scale in the room, do check that if will fit through your front door – or even window – before you buy.

If the scale drawings all seem too much like hard work, at least try to visualise it all in your head or physically move actual pieces of furniture around. Think about how you usually progress through the

Donal Colfer/Alice Clancy

space – perhaps from one door to another or from the door to a key piece of furniture, such as a sofa or hob.

Draw arrows on your graph paper to show how you move around the room, or through it if there is more than one door. Make sure that there is enough space to slide past furniture. Block off certain areas if you would prefer people not to be marching through them, such as a reading area in one corner.

There are rules as to how much space you should leave around pieces of furniture, but the size of your home and your idiosyncrasies mean that there will be some give and take here. As a guide, allow at least 45cm for a person to pass between items of furniture.

CHOOSING FURNITURE

Dermot Bannon Architects

SOFAS

Sofas are often required to be many things: a fashion statement, a comfortable place to sit, slouch and lie on, a climbing frame, a pet scratching-post and sometimes a bed. When you have children, a sofa is even more: a castle, a picnic table, a swimming pool. I caught my middle boy about to dive off our sofa, after watching the Olympics.

Think about who will use it, and how. A teen will slouch on the sofa and a person with limited mobility will find it difficult to get out of a low sofa. I've got three small children, so although I love fabric sofas, we opted for a leather one and it's been great. Cornflakes have been spilled on it and it's been turned into a 'house' by the kids. Friends of ours bought the fabric version of our leather sofa and it feels completely different.

I don't believe in getting rid of a sofa after 10 years; it should last much longer than that. We bought our first sofa when all our friends were buying new houses and getting a first-time buyer's grant. They furnished their whole houses with the FTB cheque while we bought an old house and got our first couch in an auction for £30. It did us for two years and we saved hard for the one we really wanted. We used to go and visit it in the Sofa Factory. Then the guy rang us and said they were selling a demonstration model. It was still very expensive for us, but 14 years later, the sofa looks as good as it did on the day we bought it. You can have a sofa for life.

When buying on a budget, look out for things that could fail, such as spindly legs. Make sure that they are well secured and look as if they can carry the weight of the sofa for years; otherwise choose a sofa that has shorter, fatter legs that sits near the floor (although you will then lose under-sofa storage space).

Aughey O'Flaherty Architects/Marie-Louise Halpenny

The other element that shows signs of wear and tear is the upholstery. Just as with mattresses, tightly knitted springs are the ideal, while solid foam sofas tend to sag after a while.

Ideally you want to be able to rest your back against the rear cushions while being able to bend your knees over the front, with your feet on the floor.

SUITE NIGHTMARES

I'm a big believer in not buying suites, which is something we are obsessed with in Ireland. A sofa and armchair do not need to match, and you can be much more flexible and creative if they don't. Buy things in a colour that speaks to you, something that pulls at your heart strings, rather than opting for matchy-matchy. A grey couch, for instance, will come alive with a green or orange armchair. Having a sofa in one colour and a chair in a contrasting shade works especially well with a neutral backdrop. You can also mix and match styles, such as putting a flat pack armchair with an expensive sofa.

Dermot Bannon Architects

ON OCCASION

Living rooms always need surfaces to put tea and coffee cups on. Stackable nests of occasional tables can be useful because they are portable and can be stored away, but stools can work just as well, are often cheaper and have a dual purpose. They will come in handy when you have guests over for dinner.

Another surface for putting things on is armchair and sofa armrests. If you choose one with wide, flat arms, then they will hold books and magazines (and even drinks if you don't mind living in fear of spills).

FKL Architects

STORAGE

Toys, books, a stereo system, DVDs, CDs, remote controls, spare lamp bulbs, ornaments... List all of your storage needs so that an open and closed system can be designed to neatly store everything and stop the room looking cluttered.

Peter Legge Associates

The standard choice for living rooms is a wooden (or engineered or laminate wood) floor with a rug or rugs to soften and delineate areas.

Natural timber looks and wears the best, and solid wood can always be re-sanded. Engineered boards, made from layers of wood, are usually recommended if you want underfloor heating because they are more stable in the event of temperature changes (and dampness).

Finishes include wax, varnish and oil. If one of your reasons for choosing wood is because it is natural, renewable, breathes and even eliminates pollutants, then opt for oil or natural wax to encourage this rather than sealing it with a synthetic substance. Oil and wax do not scuff either.

When choosing wooden floors you also have the option of a synthetic mix (in laminate floors), made from layers of synthetic material.

Some people still prefer wall-to-wall carpet, which is less noisy than a wooden floor but harder to keep clean. With carpets you not only get what you pay for in terms of durability, but if you skimp on quality, it often shows. Wool looks and feels good and wears well. Another option is a wool and nylon mix, or a completely synthetic carpet (including nylon, acrylic and polyester).

If you want a contemporary, natural look, consider sisal, jute, coir, seagrass or other fibres; you can even have a paper weave. Some people find them rough underfoot, while others enjoy the massage. It can be difficult to vacuum out bits of dirt that work their way through them though.

To go the Mediterranean route, you could consider floor tiles. Terracotta, slate and stone look striking, but the fear is of literally striking them – they are hard. If you opt for tiles, warm them up with underfloor heating and rugs.

LIVING ROOM RULES

▶ Find a focus: usually the TV, fire (a must-have) and/or a view. Don't let a TV dominate.

▶ Make sure the scale of your furniture matches the size of the room.

▶ Watch where you put the doors and beware of creating a through-route if there are two doors.

▶ Consider radiator positions carefully in order to fit the furniture around them. Think about underfloor heating to get rid of the problem altogether.

▶ Have a large sofa and comfortable chairs that are loosely positioned so that they can be angled for social interaction and moved for other activities, such as reading or watching TV.

▶ Have flexible lighting – dimmer switches, various lamps (rather than one overhead pendant light), wall-lights that highlight pictures and a central switch from which you can turn them all on.

Peter Legge Associates

CHAPTER 10

BEDROOMS

'You may concentrate on appearances all through the rest of your house, but in the bedroom comfort should be supreme. Bedrooms should also be very intimate – they should express your personal preferences in every way. Of all the rooms in the house, your bedroom is yours.'
– Dorothy Draper, *In the Pink*

If anywhere in the home is the place for the soul, it is the bedroom. It is where you get undressed, a place to go when you need privacy, a sanctuary when you are unwell and where you sleep, think and read. A bedroom may be the only place that partners have together.

Whatever you do there, a bedroom is the space where you get away from everything. If a house is very busy, the bedroom should be as far from the main hub as possible.

PRACTICALLY SPEAKING

....

While it is a place to sleep in – and we spend about a third of our lives there – a bedroom often does double duty to accommodate other activities. At one time or another, many of us have even worked in bedrooms, whether as students or freelancers. If you do have to have an office space in your bedroom, try to screen your desk off at night.

If the room is large enough and is carefully planned, it can incorporate other things, such as a sitting area where a couple can catch up and have a chat, or an easy chair to read in.

It should be cosy, but with all the pressure on the space from clothes, hairdryers, make-up and so on, it is in danger of becoming a cluttered nest. That is why storage needs to be carefully planned. Space-saving devices even go so far as which way the door is hung. Our predecessors, with their Victorian values, preferred to have the door open in a way that screened the room from view: not something that is on the to-do list nowadays, but it could be worth considering. But whether or not you are temporarily hiding a part of the room (or individuals in compromising positions), the door can be positioned to accommodate, and screen, storage. If possible, have about 600mm of space behind a door in which to put a wardrobe or drawers to stop them from dominating the view or room.

The bed itself should be as generously sized as you can fit. Very few people buy 4ft 6in double beds any more. The shortest dimension in a bedroom should be 2.9 metres to allow you to walk around the end of the bed. This is such a critical dimension

Robert Bourke Architects/Alice Clancy

Donaghy & Dimond Architects

that I will rob space from other areas if need be to get it to work.

Bedside tables for each occupant are crucial and they need to be big enough and close enough to ensure that the things you need (books, clock, phone, drinks) are within reach.

It's ideal to have sockets near the bed as well as the ability to turn off all lighting, from central pendants to reading lamps. It is helpful to look at how hotels have addressed bedside life – the more client-friendly sleep-sellers have thought this through (even though some still have bedside lights that are nigh on impossible to read by). Many international chains have woken up to the need for all sorts of sockets beside beds, from iPod docks to computer link-ups. This can also be done in the home – unless you are worried about electronic waves. Indeed, some eco-friendly hotels have minimal electrics in a bedroom – and won't have the wiring in a ring – to cut what they perceive to be negative electronic fields.

One activity I don't like in the bedroom is watching television. As a child I was never allowed to have one, so I never wanted one as a student at university either. Now I won't allow my own kids to have a television in their bedrooms (you can always watch programmes on a smartphone). But I am susceptible if I stay in a hotel with a television. All of the reasons why I look forward to a trip away in a hotel – peace, relaxation – are thrown out of the window if there is a television in the room. I keep watching and don't go to sleep as early as I should. I have had much more relaxing holidays in a caravan with no television.

Television and sleep don't go together for me, but I realise that this is a personal point of view; a friend of mine can't sleep unless she has the television on and has it on a timer to turn off after she has fallen asleep.

MOOD BOARD

While bedrooms are the place you go to sleep in, they are also the space you wake up in, so colours and curtains need to reflect that. While blues and greens are relaxing, yellow and white will bounce morning light around. Earthy colours, such as a warm red or honey, can be grounding and cosy. And remember that this is the one room in which you will spend a lot of time looking at the ceiling, so don't neglect that.

If you like to wake up with natural light, then if you can, put the bedroom on the east side of your home. Sleeping to the east suits us biologically: humans have a sensitive metabolic clock, and if you design a room to be in tune with your natural cycle, which is dependent on the sun, it is likely to induce the most nourishing kind of sleep. Waking to the sun not only warms you gently, but it allows you to wake up at the moment that serves you best.

Muslin curtains or pale blinds will filter natural light, creating a bright room as well as providing daytime privacy. Window treatments for bedrooms can be multilayered to account for night and day, summer and winter, with shutters or curtains adding extra warmth and darkness (keeping a room dark in the morning is also crucial for a good night's sleep for those who don't work hours that tie in with the sun).

Staying in tune with the body, which doesn't take kindly to breathing chemicals, it makes sense to have as many natural materials in a bedroom as possible – something to bear in mind when choosing bedroom furniture and finishes.

CHILDREN'S BEDROOMS

BABIES

A lot of children's room designs are defined by adults' views of what they should be. Don't buy lots of special furniture and other items for a baby, as it will be used for such a short time. Little swinging cribs, miniature wardrobes and large nappy-changing units will last for less than two years per child and Baby's too young to appreciate the fact that you've invested in mini items just for him or her.

Our babies were changed on the floor, on the bed or wherever was handy to lie them down. We didn't need to bring them to a changing depot. Babies can be changed anywhere you can lay everything out and where they have room to wriggle around.

If you are seduced by miniature or specialised furniture and pay a lot for it, you might then be tempted to hang onto these items, which will clutter your space. Good basics are a cot, a portable nappy-changing mat, a comfortable chair and a large chest of drawers.

The same goes for decorating. Nursery patterns have an incredibly short life; plain and simple is best. And don't worry about decorating the room along gender lines: a boy and a girl will happily sleep in a pink or blue (or any other colour) bedroom.

DMVF Architects/Ros Kavanagh

My sister, who is a Montessori teacher, taught me that geometric shapes in strong colours are much more stimulating to a baby than pretty, ethereal pictures in pale pink and blue, which young eyes can't register as easily. We cut out circles, squares and squiggles, laminated them and stuck them on the wall. When infants are a bit older you can cut shapes out of carpets so that they can feel the texture. A baby's room can be a springboard to creativity.

This room has to last from 0–18 months or more, so it is best if it can bring a sense of continuity through years of rapid change while also being flexible and able to accommodate each new stage of development.

NOT JUST FOR SLEEP

Bedrooms serve a different role for children in that it is also their play space. Position it with this in mind and be aware of how it connects to their play area outside (preferably a garden, but perhaps the street). The route between the two should pass between other areas they can play in – maybe a hall or corridor, a kitchen, a reception room or other children's bedrooms. Ideally, children should be able to play throughout a house, starting from their bedroom and ending outside.

TIDY-UP TIME

Storage is very important, especially from pre-school age onwards, and furniture designers have come up with many clever solutions, from platform beds with drawers and wardrobes beneath them to toy chests and dressing-up boxes that double as benches. Space for sleepovers, including pull-out beds (from beneath a sofa or another bed), is also important.

SCHOOLCHILDREN

At this stage of a child's life the bedroom starts to become a social centre, so you can introduce bean bags, floor rugs and other friendly furniture for them to sit on and move around. They also start to become interested in clothes, design and self-expression, which may require a wardrobe, where perhaps they formerly had their clothes in drawers, so that they can see their clothes clearly and choose what to wear themselves.

TEENAGERS

As they negotiate the threshold between childhood and becoming an adult, teens need a room that gives them autonomy and privacy. Teenagers will want to decorate their own room at this stage with pictures, strings of lights and so on. But the look is likely to be a hybrid between staying on top of trends and keeping certain things from their childhood as they leave one stage of life and start the next. What they need from you now is support as they explore their self and boundaries, reflecting on who they are – the ever-changing answer to which will probably manifest in the design of the room. Judge it and you risk judging them.

BATHROOMS

THE POWER OF WATER

Water is a very powerful element, which humans love to sink into and need to drink. Our bodies are 90 per cent water and it is vital for our survival. The effects of coming into direct contact with water through bathing and showering – and thus being in contact with nature and our natural instincts – should not be underestimated. You can see that children love water, and whatever children love tends to be the right thing for the human soul.

One of the simplest ways of unwinding is by taking a bath, something that cultures around the world have celebrated, from being immersed into the Ganges River in India, to scrub-downs in Japanese bathhouses, to playing chess in Hungarian thermal baths and bathing in Bath itself.

Bathing has been both a solitary and communal ritual throughout history and right up to today, as families and friends gather for saunas (sweating out their own water and plunging into cool pools) or come together on beaches. Whether alone or with others, bathing has an intimacy and a paring back to our souls, not least from the removal of clothes.

HOW MANY BATHROOMS DO YOU NEED?

Bathrooms in many modern homes have shrunk and become more efficient. The thinking goes that if you can have a shower in five minutes, then so much the better. It reflects how life has changed along with the way in which we use bathrooms. Yet we need to remember how important a bathroom is. We have slightly lost touch with our requirement for relaxation, and many bathrooms now are not relaxing spaces.

Donaghy & Dimond Architects/Dennis Gilbert

Our obsession with the number of bathrooms we can fit into a home has not helped, as the emphasis is on how many rather than how big. It really is worth having one large bathroom as a relaxing space and then focusing on how many en suites you can squeeze in after allocating that. One main bathroom and an en suite for the main bedroom are probably enough, or even two main bathrooms.

Something we have done on a couple of projects is that instead of an en suite, we have put two bathrooms beside each other. This works well in a house with many people, perhaps a couple and teenagers, because it can accommodate five or six people showering, shaving and so on in the morning. Having the bathrooms – one large and

one small, perhaps – side by side means people aren't marching through a private domain to have a shower, as they would with an en suite. This also works really well in holiday homes, with the added advantage of people being able to easily wash themselves down when they come in from the beach.

Having bathrooms beside each other is also efficient as far as services are concerned. The cost per square metre for a bathroom is far more than any other part of the house. In terms of the budget, getting rid of a superfluous en suite can save money and effort, helping to get a building project to site.

Lawrence and Long Architects/Marie-Louise Halpenny

BATHROOM BASICS

THE BATH

I think every home should have one and be generous with it. A bath should be at least 1700mm long, but if you can extend that to 1800mm it feels much more luxurious, even though the cost difference between the sizes is negligible.

Freestanding baths look great in big bathrooms and will work if you are converting a bedroom in an old house, for instance. Beside a window is the perfect spot.

If you don't have the space, play with how the surround looks and how the bath sits in

the room. There is no longer any need to just screw on a plastic panel – you can have tiles, timber and so on. Another idea is to have a skirting board with LED lights in it so that it looks as if the bath is floating.

If you want underwater jets, remember that not all whirlpool baths are the same. Some large baths have lots of jets that are quite weak; my preference would be for fewer jets that are stronger. If you opt for a bath with three or four powerful jets, you will get the therapeutic benefits of a massage.

SHOWER

Put in as big a shower as possible, especially if there is no bath and the shower is your main contact with water. It needs to be the best experience it can be. And invest in the best showerhead you can, with the fastest flow. This does depend on good water pressure, so if you don't have enough, think about investing in a pump.

DMVF Architects/Ros Kavanagh

My big bugbear is corner showers in rooms that don't need them, as they tend to make the space feel really small and tight. Or sometimes you see a massive bathroom with a tiny shower in the corner.

For every shower tray, there's always a bigger version. You might have to wait a couple of weeks for it to be delivered, but it is worth it and the cost of a large shower tray is little more than the price of a smaller one.

If you plan in an efficient way, you can have a walk-in shower. Having this behind a glass screen, which dispenses with the need for clunky shower doors, can make a bathroom feel really luxurious and spacious.

Donal Colfer/Alice Clancy

When planning a shower, leave little alcoves in the wall for things like shampoo bottles, otherwise they all end up sitting in the shower tray or on various holders dangling from shower walls and screens. Have the recess at eye level so you don't have to bend down to look for things with water spraying all over you.

BASINS

There are so many different varieties and styles, but the key thing is to keep it really, really simple. A good basin should have 20 years of life, so don't go for what's fashionable. We often joke about avocado bathroom suites and sinks shaped like shells, but they were trendy once.

The utmost in luxury is an under-mounted sink set into a vanity unit. With the basin under-mounted and stone on top, you get a nice big countertop for all your lotions and potions, shaving paraphernalia or make-up.

If the vanity unit and space are big enough, you can put in a second sink. In the last few years there has been a trend for over-mounted basins, but it doesn't leave as much space around the basin and you have to be frugal with what items you put on top.

If space is so tight that you can't have a standard vanity unit, the next option is a semi-recessed unit where the cupboards are narrow and the basin sticks out beyond the unit.

If you don't have a vanity unit, a wall-hung basin will give a small bathroom a great feeling of space because nothing touches the ground, making the floor area appear bigger. You will need to put a support in the wall to hang the basin from.

Pedestals are still around, but all the pedestal does is give the impression that it is holding the sink and it hides pipes. But if you plan the bathroom early enough and put the waste pipe into the wall, you can have a much smarter-looking basin.

Donaghy & Dimond Architects/Luke White

WCs

If you can, conceal the cistern for a cleaner look and to free up space. You can sit it in a vanity unit, along with the sink, or conceal it in a wall if you can. A lift-off flat plate allows you to service the cistern if need be.

Of the different types of toilet pans, a wall-hung one is usually the best option. In smaller bathrooms it uses the space efficiently and makes it feel bigger. Attached with steel brackets and two arms that hold the toilet, a wall-hung toilet appears to float off the ground. As with wall-hung basins, the floor flows underneath. This makes it more hygienic too, as you can mop under the toilet and there are no nooks or crannies.

Dermot Bannon Architects/Enda Cavanagh

Donal Colfer/Alice Clancy

If you are using a toilet with a visible cistern, place it right back to the wall for a neater look.

In bathrooms that don't have space for a vanity unit or support for a wall-hung toilet, there are really compact toilets with simple shapes. It is worth spending the extra few euro for something that looks as simple as possible.

When choosing sanitary ware people often think they have to buy designer brands, but simplicity is the key to it all and such products can be found in all price ranges. Where you do need to spend money is on taps and fittings, such as door handles, that you touch every day.

When we were doing up our bathroom before we moved into our house, my wife, who was in charge of money, gave me a budget for the tap. I really wanted one of Arne Jacobsen's Vola taps and negotiated a discount with a supplier I'd often worked with, but it was still double the budget. That didn't stop me. I bought the tap and kept it hidden under the bed – as if it were 'tap porn' – in case she found it. She still doesn't know how much that tap cost: it was spread out over a couple of credit cards. Yet every time I use that tap, even 10 years later, I still smile. When we move, it is coming with us.

Dermot Bannon Architects/Enda Cavanagh

HOT TOPIC

Put in a towel rail that also operates as a radiator. Some even have a switch-on element in them so that they can be used when the central heating is turned off, so you can have warm towels in the summer without having to turn on the heating.

UPGRADE

After the kitchen, upgrading a bathroom is one area that will really add value to a home. Many bathrooms are poorly laid out, so rather than just going out and buying a new suite, look at the layout of the bathroom and think about how it can be improved. If you have lived with it for a while, you will probably know this instinctively.

PG Architects/Peter Cook

Lots of bathroom brochures have graph paper and templates so that you can draw in where the window(s) and door are and cut out the templates to see how they fit (leaving enough space to move around them).

When considering changing things around, remember that the most expensive thing to relocate is the toilet because it needs to be beside a soil-vent pipe, and moving one of these is a major task. Showers and basins are fed by smaller pipes, so they are more portable (although a walk-in shower will possibly require floor upheaval).

When shopping for new bathroom fittings, check the water pressure needed to use them. You may need to install a pump or buy taps and showerheads that can work with a lower pressure.

EN SUITES AND WET ROOMS

Planning in advance, and efficiently, will allow you to make great use of space in an en suite. By having sliding doors or an outward opening door, for instance, you can fit in a bigger shower and leave a proper space for a toilet.

When staying in Scandinavian hotels, I've marvelled at how some of them get bathrooms that work efficiently into really small spaces. They are often wet rooms, which hone space by dispensing with shower trays. Wet rooms have a trap in the floor into which all the water runs: the whole room acts like a shower tray. Often they will

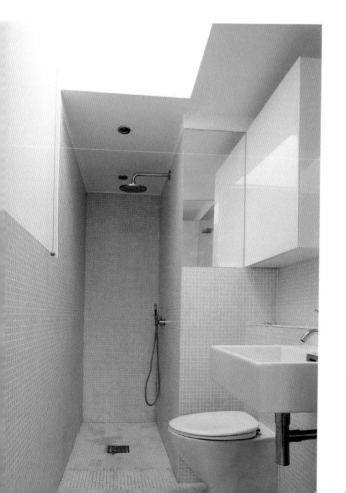

Peter Legge Associates

Donaghy & Dimond Architects/Marie-Louise Halpenny

Donaghy & Dimond Architects/Luke White

Ailtireacht

have a double-layered floor, perhaps using a strip of fibreglass, for extra waterproofing.

Wet rooms can also be handy places, especially if they are downstairs, to wash various things down, including pets, buggy wheels and rollerblades!

LIGHTING

Lighting is really important in a bathroom. We've all been a bit lazy about this and put up with one central light. Yet lighting can be used to create a relaxed atmosphere, or conversely to create well-lit areas for applying make-up, shaving and so on by having a task light above a mirror.

LED strip lighting is great for creating a relaxing and somewhat dramatic mood. It can be used on top of storage – something we did in a house in Dun Laoghaire between the top of the built-in storage and the ceiling. LED lights can also be used to create a floating effect (very appropriate in a bathroom!) by running along low-placed strips, such as beneath a bath.

One thing you don't want above a bath is a bright light glaring down at you: bathroom lights should be dimmable.

With such varied lighting, you should be able to switch each one on and off separately. Having flexible lighting doesn't cost a whole lot more than standard lighting, and yet it changes how a place feels and increases its usability.

Peter Legge Associates

STORAGE

·····························

If you don't have a vanity unit, it is important to have some kind of storage unit, either against the wall or built in. Not everything needs to be hidden: sort out what you want on display. Pretty bottles of products and perfumes liven up a bathroom and it is useful to have everything close to hand rather than having to scrabble in the back of cupboards for everything.

Having a place to put things away means you can buy 400 toilet rolls on special offer and have somewhere to put spare towels and all those children's bath toys, from ducks to plastic whales that pull apart, that we seem to have in our house.

Ailtireacht

Dermot Bannon Architects/Enda Cavanagh

MATERIALS

Keep bathroom materials simple to create a calm backdrop for all those things you have in the bathroom, from shower gels to the wherewithal to cleanse, tone and moisturise.

Along with simplicity, which will help the bathroom feel bigger too, try to keep the materials as natural as possible. Among their many benefits, using stone, clay and timber chimes well with the natural element of water. Wood is great when introduced in a vanity unit, built-in furniture and as a worktop. When tiling, I really like to use the same tiling material on the floor and wall (check the slip

Dermot Bannon Architects/Enda Cavanagh

rating when buying tiles). Stone can look fantastic too. It gives bathrooms a sumptuous feel and ages well, so it is worth it if the budget runs to it.

A step down from that is porcelain, which differs from ceramic (next in line) in that the colour runs the whole way through. This means it can have its edge exposed and negates the need for an edge tile. A simple ceramic tile in a plain colour can also look great. Be adventurous!

Mosaic tiles look good, especially in small spaces, and they can look amazing in striking colours in a wet room. In wet rooms, the floor has a slight slope, which often makes it difficult to accommodate large tiles. Again, mosaic on the floor can run up the walls.

Another floor type worth considering in bathrooms is rubber, which comes in all sorts of colours, from muted to bright.

FKL Architects/Verena Hilgenfeld

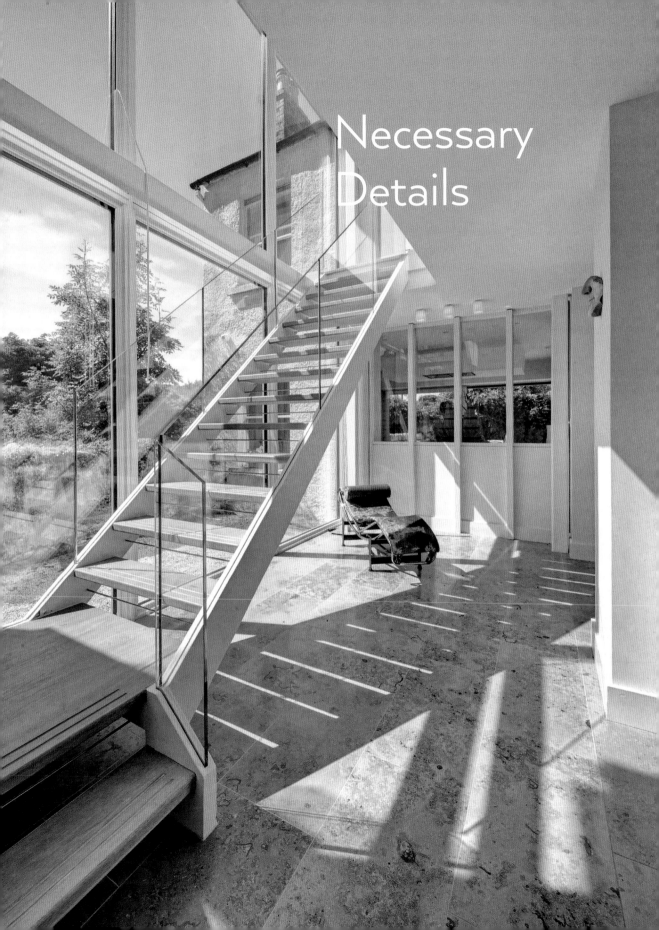

Necessary
Details

CHAPTER 12

IDENTIFYING YOUR NEEDS

THE BRIEF

A good brief is important because there are so many different design solutions to every problem – probably five or six. And it is crucial to find your own solution, one that answers your needs.

That's why I don't like it when people say they want a design that I did for someone else. In order for me to design something that really suits a person, I need to have their brief. We have become so accustomed to wanting something we have seen before or to making our home similar to a neighbour's. You have to want more of yourself for yourself.

I love it when my clients say a home really works for them, and the reason why that happened is because they made a wish list and I responded to their specific needs. Time spent at the start analysing everything is crucial to a great project. Good design is only as good as a good brief. It gives parameters for an architect to work within. The first thing I do is talk to clients about their lifestyle and how they use a home. People's needs differ hugely. Some love to cook, some don't. Some like to entertain, some don't. Even if there is just a couple in the home, theirs may be the place that the extended family often descends on for gatherings.

Ryan Kennihan Architects/Alice Clancy

Then there are hobbies. If people do lots of water sports, they need somewhere to hang wetsuits. Ditto with golf clubs – where will they be stored? Does someone look after the local football team and have up to 15 sets of kit that need to be washed? Do you go for family walks with an all-terrain buggy that gets muddy wheels? In a holiday home, do you need a place to wash off sand after a day at the beach?

Putting such things on a wish list will result in a house that responds to your needs rather than having you curse muddy tyre marks on a beautiful timber floor near the main door or putting up with wetsuits drying on garden furniture.

In my childhood home there were often bowls of strawberry mousse sitting all the way up the stairs. My mum, a home economics teacher, made them each week for Meals on Wheels but she had nowhere to store them. It illustrates how if something like this is a regular part of your life, your home needs to be reconfigured. My mum could have had a long worktop or shelves for all those lovely pink desserts. And then there was the way my mum laid out fabric and dress patterns on the floor when she was sewing, and how she had to move furniture around in the dining room when she was marking papers. If she had redesigned the house, this could have become a study and an integral part of working life.

John Feely Architects/Ros Kavanagh

FKL Architects/Verena Hilgenfeld

ROOM FOR ACTIVITY

Think about activities and look at the actual function of each room and how you want them to feel. In the living room, will you primarily be watching television or will you not have one at all? Is the dining room used every day or just at weekends? Is the home office used all the time or just twice a week? Honing this will mean spending less money because you won't be putting in loads of rooms you don't need.

At the start of the project, do a diary of a day in your house. Again, this goes back to the point about people saying they want the same as the house up the road, whereas what I really need to know is how *you* live. This way, important things will not be overlooked. Look at what happens on weekdays – is anyone in the house during the day? Also look at a Saturday or Sunday when everybody is at home – which parts of the house become congested? Is there a lot of activity in the kitchen in the morning? Does that room need to be on the east side for morning sun? A diary helps me to locate rooms for my client.

Discuss what you like and don't like in your existing home. Walk through it and say what works or doesn't work in each space. Also keep in mind why you are doing the building work: what is the reason for a reconfiguration, a new extension or a new house? Is the current kitchen too small? Do you need more bedrooms? More living space?

Consider the size you expect each room to be. This is a good time to visit family, friends' and neighbours' homes: stand in rooms and see if

they feel right. An architect will help you with this, whether you go and stand in other homes or not!

List any rooms that you don't use and why. Perhaps they are too small or they are an awkward distance from the living space, down at the end of a corridor and not worth the bother. Such rooms could be reinvented as something else: a playroom, music room, spare bedroom or even all three. Dining rooms can often be reinvented as something else. Or a big utility room might suit a large family, helping them survive the day-to-day grind, better than a guest bedroom.

WORKING TOGETHER

Draw Venn diagrams, putting each room in its own bubble and deciding which ones need to be beside each other: perhaps the living room beside the kitchen beside the utility and then the laundry.

If you are putting in a spare bedroom, think carefully about who will use it. Is there someone who visits regularly with specific requirements? Is it easy to negotiate with a walking frame or wheelchair? Perhaps the bedroom should be downstairs. Consider specific needs for any other rooms in the house.

FEELING GOOD

Having considered your needs, now consider your wants, your feelings, the things that matter to you. Energy efficiency could be a priority, or maybe technology is your thing: would you like built-in speakers? What are your lighting requirements?

Bring out your creative side with a mood board, which will guide you towards paint colours and furnishings that will really speak to you. Most people who are doing any kind of renovation will have stacks of interiors and architectural magazines beside their beds. It's time to be a bit less precious with these and start tearing out the

Sterrin O'Shea Architects

pages. If you find that you have ripped out 400 sheets, maybe start on things that you *don't* like. The mood board will reveal themes and schemes, showing not only you but also your architect how you would like the house to feel.

Designing for your lifestyle will make it into your home: it's as much about your needs as your taste.

CHAPTER 13

BUDGETING

Before you start, draw up a wish list of everything you want and put things in order of priority. You may have to be ruthless about items lower down the list and forfeit them if things get tight. Be realistic about what you can afford to spend without stretching yourself.

Think long term about your project. Will you only be spending four or five years in your home and then moving on, or is this a house for life? You can spend more money on the house of your dreams: it is better to do all that you can now than to revisit the project in five years' time.

Add fees to the list, remembering that additional work may be needed once the build is on site and issues come up. A good amount to hold back for contingencies is 15 per cent, but do keep back at least 8–10 per cent. Once you have taken out the amount for contingencies and the fees for building work, you'll be left with a realistic budget.

With this budget in mind, you can draw up the initial design. If you are building an extension you also need to factor in the existing house – there is no point constructing an amazing extension and not upgrading the building it is attached to. At the very least, this could involve redoing plumbing, electrics, insulation and windows. Sometimes when significant work is done to the existing house, it can cost two-thirds of the price of a regular build.

Garbhan Doran Architects

A good place to start with is on the house you have in order to work out how much you need to spend on that. Subtract this sum from the overall figure to give the type of extension that you are able to build. Bear in mind that if the extension will contain a kitchen or bathroom, it is likely to be more expensive than one with a living room or bedroom because the former are highly serviced.

Sit down and really think about which rooms you are in for most of the time, and spend the most money on these. If you spend a lot of time in the kitchen, there is no point buying high-end materials for the bedrooms.

At this stage, if it is a big project, such as an entire new house, it may be worth taking on a quantity surveyor, who will give you a more firm idea of initial costs. QS costs depend on how much you require them to do: a cost plan will cost a couple of hundred euro, whereas if you want the whole job looking after, it will run to a couple of thousand euro. If you are doing a substantial job, then it is worth employing a QS for the entire project.

Aughey O'Flaherty Architects/Marie-Louise Halpenny

TENDER LOVING CARE

········

It is certainly worth getting a cost plan done before applying for planning permission, as there is no point in getting permission for something that you can't afford to build. At this stage you should allocate parts of the budget to specific areas. Look at the exact materials you will use and what they cost. You might want a high-end kitchen or a beautiful stone on the hall floor or timber on the living room floor, but is it too expensive?

The budget is actually a key part of the design process – it is as important as the brief. It will also be fluid. At certain times in the design process you may go over budget, and as you add things in, you can draw back on others if need be. Eventually you will have a comprehensive set of tender drawings.

John Feely Architects/Ros Kavanagh

When you are asking builders to pitch for the job, make sure that the tender document you give them lists absolutely everything that is going into the build, including fixtures and fittings. The more comprehensive the list, the more realistic the figures will be. Ambiguities in the document will lead to ambiguities in the costing. And the more sure you are of the final price, the easier it is to stay within the budget. It can be an arduous process, but by putting in the time and effort at this stage, the time on site will be much smoother and you will be much more sure of costs. People often leave a lot of things out of the planning permission drawings, use them for tendering and then wonder why costs have spiralled out of control.

Another thing that needs to be factored into the budget at this stage is that when planning permission comes back, you might have to pay a planning contribution, which can run from a couple of thousand euro to around €15,000. For many local authorities, this planning contribution is a condition of getting planning. It is more relevant in new builds, but sometimes we've been asked for it for house extensions.

BUILDING CONFIDENCE

When going out to tender, contact at least four, or even five, builders, because when you get the prices back you will have a good spread. If four are very similar and one is very low or high, then you can be pretty sure that there is something wrong with that figure. If you only approach two builders and one comes back with a high quote and one

has a low one, how do you know which is right or wrong? If you go to lots of contractors, then by the law of averages you can start to see a pattern.

When appointing a builder, it is vital to choose the right one, preferably someone who has come recommended and whose standard of work you have seen. It is also very important that the builder is someone you feel comfortable with and can talk openly with, because misunderstandings and miscommunication can cost money.

THE DOTTED LINE

When appointing builders, always sign a contract. I've often had clients who think this is a very formal thing to do, especially if the builder is a friend, but it is your only security if something goes wrong. You'd never consider buying a new car without a warranty, so why would you do that with your home?

Ailbríeacht

PG Architects/Peter Cook

One thing the contract does is set out rules for payments to the builder. Before starting on site, ask the builder for a schedule of payment, which gives a breakdown of what he thinks will be required month by month. This will help you make sure you have the funds available, because if it is, say, a six-month build, the payments are unlikely to be the same each month. If the windows are going in on month three, then you may need to double the payments that month. If you are borrowing from a bank you can give this outline to the lender so that they can organise the funds. While banks won't release the money until you obtain a certificate of payment, it is worth having the cash flow organised and keeping everyone in the picture.

You always pay a builder in arrears for their work, never upfront, because if something happens, then you haven't handed over money for work that hasn't been done.

SMOOTH RUNNING

Try to make as few changes as possible once a project goes on site. Alterations cost money, and 10 seemingly small decisions can push a budget up by thousands of euro. But having said that, sometimes great opportunities present themselves and these should not be ignored.

Don't delay decisions on site, as this will hold up your builder and incur costs. It pays to plan ahead. Make sure that all the finishes and fittings you have picked can be delivered to fit in with the builder's schedule. If something is going to take six weeks to deliver and doesn't fit the on-site schedule, then you may have to choose another item, as delays cost money.

Dermot Bannon Architects/Enda Cavanagh

CHOOSE CAREFULLY

Each decision can push costs up hugely, so it really does pay to shop around – the legwork can save you serious money. But don't scrimp on quality when it comes to the things you are going to use every day, such as taps and sanitary ware. I learned this in my own house, where I had to replace a kitchen tap three times before finally spending extra on a good-quality one. There is normally a reason for bargain-basement prices, unless you know the product has been genuinely discounted from a substantially higher price.

As you buy things, keep the receipts in one place because when you buy appliances and carpets separately on various cards, you can forget what you have spent. By keeping everything together, you will always be aware of your actual budget.

DELAYED GRATIFICATION

If you need to cut costs, don't scrimp on the 'shell and core', or structural, items. Windows and insulation, for instance, are things that you can't go back and do again (without huge disruption and cost). Sometimes people will change the window specification from timber to PVC because it saves a few thousand euro – I've often been in situations where this was done to pay for a swanky television. If money is tight, I highly recommended allocating funds to core items such as windows, insulation or electrics. You don't even have to floor out a room, put in skirting or paint it. Phase the project in order of importance and wait to get the things you don't need right now.

CHAPTER 14

PLANNING PERMISSION

Planning in this country is often treated as some kind of enigma; people think it would be easier to break into the Vatican than get planning permission. It is often even referred to with a definite article: '*the* planning'.

In a country where 92 per cent of one-off houses are not designed by architects but by builders and developers, planners have been trying to protect the landscape and built environment, and when they are not dealing with a designer they tend to come down a bit heavy. Because people didn't

use architects, planners have been battling and guarding against poor-quality design for years. Yet with a bit of insight, you can achieve a great home that planners will love and that you will love, and which won't be a blot on the landscape.

The first port of call, especially when building a new house, is to look at the local development control plan, which will tell you what category the land is zoned under. In some cases the prospective house-builders will have to meet local needs criteria and prove they have a strong

connection to the area. For instance, it could be that they have lived in the area for a long time, have relatives there, have a business that benefits the locality or are involved in beneficial farming.

However, just because someone has a plot of land, or their parents have a plot, does not necessarily mean they meet the local needs requirement. It helps to approach planning in a sensitive way – which has not always been the case. The attitude has often been, 'Ireland is our home – why should we be dictated to by local authorities?' A big problem was this notion that we were connected to the field, that it was our land and we should be able to do what we wanted with it.

Aughey O'Flaherty Architects/Marie-Louise Halpenny

The planning process can actually be straightforward if it is followed methodically. When entering the process, you need to show you have the best intentions, and if you have good, creative architecture, you will be surprised at what planners will allow. If they appreciate and understand where you are coming from, they will help guide you through the planning process.

DO I NEED PLANNING PERMISSION?

If you are building a new home it will always require planning permission, but if you want to do a small job on a house, certain projects don't need permission. These exempt developments are generally small in scale and don't affect the nature of the street. They include garage conversions and an extension to the rear of the house that is under 40 square metres. If the house has been extended before (after 1964 in Ireland), the size of that has to be subtracted from the 40 square metres.

Some of the allocation (12 square metres) can be used as a room on top of the extension, but this has to be at least 2 metres from boundaries. The extension has to leave at least 25 square metres of garden, although there are certain exemptions to this; check with your planning authority. Any windows at ground level on an extension should be 1 metre or more from the boundary, and on the first floor they have to be 11 metres away.

PG Architects/Peter Cook

You can also build a porch without planning permission if it is less than 2 square metres, but do check with the development plan that it isn't in a conservation area. It's also worth checking legal maps. Ten years ago I drew up a porch for a house, but it turned out there was a right of way right up against all of the houses' fronts on the terrace because their front gardens were so long the postman was given the right to hop over all of the front garden walls. Legally we couldn't build the porch because it blocked this access.

Sterrin O'Shea Architects

PRE-PLANNING MEETING

....

Once you buy a site, or even beforehand, it is worth having a conversation with the planners about whether you are allowed to build there before doing drawings. It could save a fortune. You just won't be able to build in some areas, regardless of what the design is like.

If the local development plan shows that you are in a conservation area and/or the house is a protected structure, then it will restrict what you can do to an existing house – for instance, you will need to keep the front elevation intact.

It is worth engaging with planners at different stages of the project, so once there are clear initial sketches, you should set up a meeting with them. This helps get rid of that enigma around planning. Bring models and 3-Ds, if they are available, to discuss the project with. This saves loads of time and sorts out any issues in advance.

Apart from the design itself, planners will be able to highlight any issues concerning infrastructure, such as sewers, drainage, access where it may not be possible to see cars coming along the road and so on. This will indicate areas that may cause permission to be refused. Dealing with planners in advance like this will also stop them issuing requests for additional information. Some of these can be a surprise, such as not allowing a window in a certain place.

This liaison with local authorities happens in various ways. Some of them meet applicants in person, others correspond by email and others will chat on the phone (or a variety of all three), but they are all open to engagement.

GOOD NEIGHBOURS

After the planners have agreed in principle to a design, it's a good idea to talk to the neighbours. Few people like change, especially in the house next door, so drop in plans and go through any issues and concerns they have. Ninety per cent of the time neighbours won't have an issue with your plans, but they will get concerned if they see a site notice and will wonder what is going on. I'd like to be kept in the picture if my neighbours were doing work. Being open and transparent with neighbours also helps relations. It's not worth falling out with them over an extension, but I see it happening over and over again, and nine times out of 10 it's because of non-communication.

Neighbours might ask for something, such as a wall to be lowered, and if you do compromise it makes the whole process much easier. If the neighbours are happy, they are less likely to appeal against the application and hold you up.

NOTICE

As part of the planning process, you have to put a notice in a newspaper. If you plan this in advance, you can save lots of money: a local newspaper will run the ad for about €12 in some cases, whereas a national newspaper will charge €300 or €400. Ask the local authority which newspapers you can use. If you're pushed for time you will have to use a national paper, as they can publish the notice the following day, whereas a local paper might need to have the ad booked a week in advance of publication.

A site notice also needs to be put up and kept in place for five weeks. If it comes down for any reason – if it is stolen, perhaps – it must be replaced very quickly, otherwise the application can be deemed invalid.

PERMISSION GRANTED

After five to eight weeks, the local authority will make its decision on the application. They may request further information, but hopefully not because you will have sorted out all the issues in a pre-planning meeting. Then there is an additional four-week period in which appeals can be made.

When planning comes through it may have certain conditions attached. Read the document carefully because the design may have to change slightly to comply with certain conditions.

Once you have been granted planning permission, it is valid for five years.

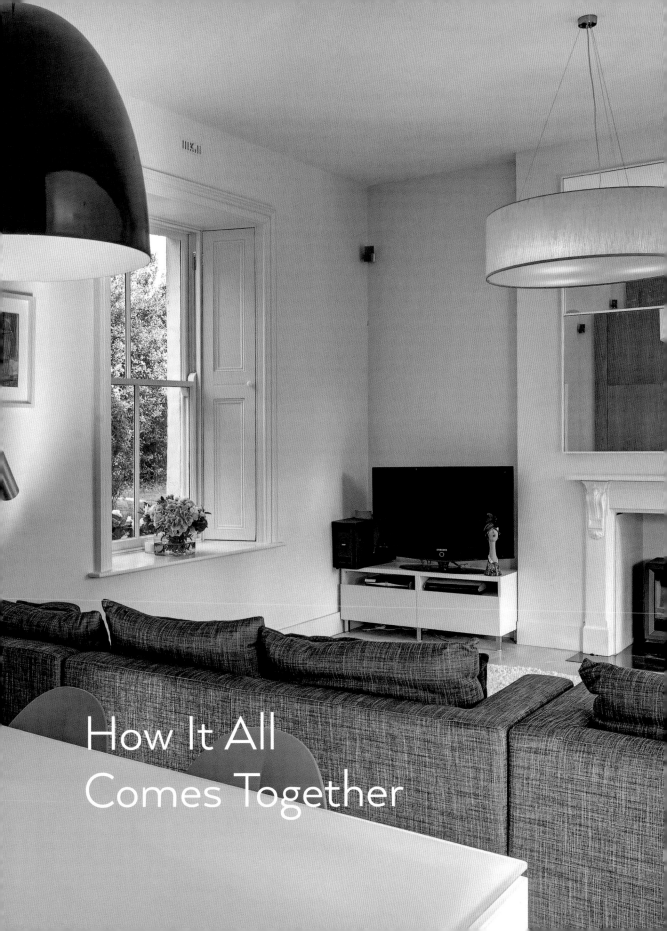

How It All
Comes Together

CHAPTER 15

CASE STUDY

THE SITE

Our clients were a couple who owned this site, had
always lived in the area, in the Irish countryside,
and wanted to build a house for them and their
five children. They chose a beautiful spot – a site
that would have been known in my college as a
'no-fail site' because it has so much going for it.
To the south is a gentle slope down to a river, to
the west are woods, to the north are hedgerows
and a lane and to the east is a tiny, typical country
road, with grass growing up its middle in places –
the natural boundaries were lovely. But while the
south-facing aspect was beautiful and sunny, it
was quite exposed and the wind blew up from the
river.

THE CLIENTS

The clients had already got planning permission
for a bungalow on the site, which they had applied
for because they originally thought that this was
the only type of building that would be allowed.
Yet they had chosen the site so well – it is a very
special place – and they knew in their hearts that
the generic bungalow didn't do justice to it. They
also felt that the building wasn't going to suit the
needs of them and their five children. Thinking
that they could do better, they approached us and
asked if we could come and have a look at the
project.

THE BRIEF

....

The couple wanted a large family space with a kitchen at its heart as the fulcrum of family life. In the same space they wanted a living room to hang out in together, and their dream was to have a dining area that felt a bit separate from these two – for Sunday dinners, family lunches and so on – yet somehow connected.

They also wanted a separate living room as an adults-only space. They said that this should also ideally be connected to the main kitchen/living space. It was the same with the playroom, as they wanted the kids to have their own space but also to be near the central zone of the house. They didn't want this room to be too big because they knew the children would outgrow it, and when they did, it was to be adaptable so that it could become another space in the future.

Ryan Kennihan Architects

Another adaptable room they requested was a study that would be large enough to become a guest bedroom if needed. For this reason, and also to have a downstairs bathroom, a shower room was to be placed beside it (not as an en suite). They requested that the two rooms be downstairs so that anyone staying over could be in a separate zone to the family. Outdoor accommodation was to include a garage and storage space for fuel and timber.

Continuing the zoning theme upstairs, the couple wanted the main bedroom, complete with walk-in wardrobe and en suite, to be slightly separate from the children's rooms. Although

they had five children, they only wanted three bedrooms because when she was a child, our client had shared rooms at certain times and she had found it to be an enriching experience. These three rooms were to be interchangeable, accommodating, at various times, up to three beds in one room and one bed in another (although knowing children, they would certainly spend the occasional night all huddled up in one room when given the chance as well as relishing times alone).

It was suggested that these be two very large bedrooms and one double, which all shared wardrobe spaces, utility/laundries and en suites – almost Jack and Jill style, undulating.

LAYING OUT THE DESIGN

....

We started with the car. In this day and age, you cannot avoid it. Nobody likes to look at vehicles out of their front window, even if it does mean convenience. So we began with the drive, which we ran tight up against the boundary and along the north-east side of the house. Here, at the side, we created an entrance courtyard where up to four cars could be parked without being seen from the main rooms. Yet they are near both the front door and another side door we created that has an entry to the utility room and laundry area. This

informal entrance was to be used by the family for shopping and discarding wet outdoor gear and so on.

We followed the sun to create this house, so the kitchen and living area at the heart of the house face south, towards the river, through a huge glass wall. This kitchen/living space is in a rectangle with the kitchen at the back of it, from where anyone preparing food can stand at the island unit and see the view. They can also join in or appreciate what's happening in the living area between the kitchen and glass wall/garden.

In answer to the clients' wishes, the playroom is to the side of the living area, to the east, and is

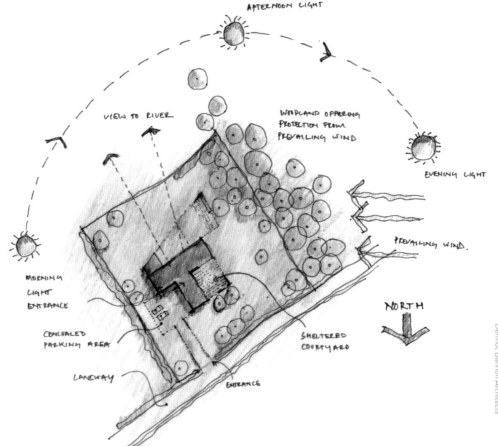

Dermot Bannon Architects

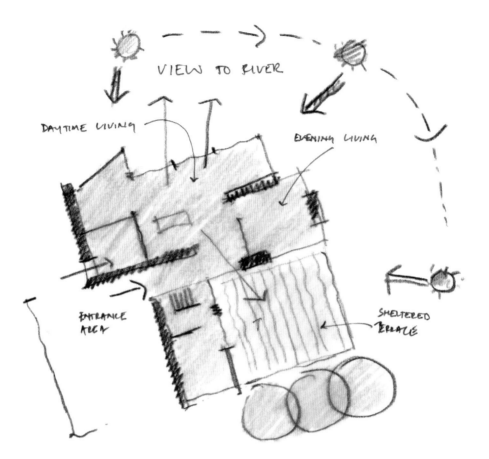

VIEW TO RIVER

DAYTIME LIVING

EVENING LIVING

ENTRANCE AREA

SHELTERED TERRACE

Dermot Bannon Architects

accessed via a sliding door. This not only works as a hangout for the kids but also as a place to store toys in. When the children are older it will revert to a morning space where people can sit and bask in the sun rising in the east.

On the other side of the living room, to the south-west, we placed a huge fireplace, which doubles up as a barrier to the dining space. This is a half screen that enables, from the dining room, diagonal views back to the kitchen (there is also a sliding door here). It is very much part of the kitchen, but when the lights are dimmed in the kitchen it feels like a separate dining room. So you get the formal dining room without wasting space

because it flows into the whole area. While this is very much part of the open-plan space, it can be sectioned off, like the playroom, by a sliding door. The same goes for the adult's living zone beside the dining room, again fulfilling the brief.

The dining room and adult's living room form two sides of a small courtyard on the southern side of the house, but while the orientation is perfect for sun it can get windy, with breezes travelling up the slope across the lawn to the glazed wall. So we created the main courtyard on the south-west side, to the front of the house. This patio is protected from the weather by woods and the house itself. With one edge of the dual-aspect

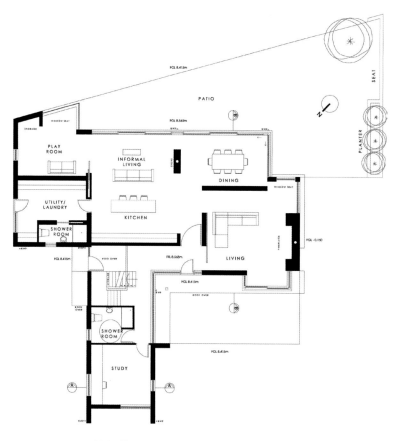

PROPOSED GROUND FLOOR PLAN

Dermot Bannon Architects

adult living room forming one side (with a bay window popping out into the space) and the study/shower room in a north wing forming the other, along with low-level planting along another edge, it is a sheltered, private courtyard providing a natural place to sit in the afternoon and evening.

When it is windy on the south side of the building, the glazing still offers the lovely view and sun, but if you have friends over for a barbecue it is less about the view and more about socialising, and that is when the south-west courtyard provides a happy, gale-free alternative. There is also a canopy over part of it.

Beside this courtyard is the wing containing the study/guest bedroom with the shower beside it. This places the study in the most private part of the house and also enables it to double up as a separate guest wing.

The entrance hall, opening to the main courtyard, is a double-height void that links both floors and brings in natural light to lots of areas. Upstairs it acts as a light well between the main bedroom in one wing and the children's bedrooms in the other (as well as bringing south-western light down from the sky to the front door).

N

17350

FLAT ROOF

ₒRWP

RWPₒ

RWPₒ

BEDROOM 1

EN-SUITE

BEDROOM 2

16750

EN-SUITE

FFL 11.325

ROOF LIGHTS OVER

WARDROBE / STORAGE

WARDROBE / STORAGE

MASTER BEDROOM

FFL 11.325

ₒRWP

RWPₒ

ₒRWP

B

ROOF LIGHTS OVER VOID

BRIDGE

ROOF BELOW

ROOF BELOW

EN-SUITE

B

DRESSING ROOM

BEDROOM 3

A

A

FFL 11.325

RWPₒ

ₒRWP

PROPOSED FIRST FLOOR PLAN

Dermot Bannon Architects

The main bedroom, with its en suite and dressing room, is in the same wing as the ground-floor study/guest room: the quiet zone. The children are in a 'loud wing', with the two larger rooms at each end and a double room in the middle. Between each bedroom is a 'service zone' with en suites, walk-in wardrobes and other storage. These zones create noise buffers, giving peace to children who are studying or sleeping. The wing can be opened up to allow you to walk from room to room, or separate areas can be shut off.

GARAGE

The garage also serves a dual purpose. It not only houses cars, but it is placed in such a way that it encloses the back courtyard and screens neighbours.

FORM

The clients wanted something that looked traditional, so this house has mainly pitched roofs (with some flat parts). Because the previous planning permission was for a bungalow, there was a height restriction. We decided to lower the building into the site, taking advantage of a natural gradient on the site. We were convinced we could get a storey and a half under the same ridge height as a bungalow. We squeezed it until we got this, with no wasted space – for instance, the lowest part of the roof reached the tops of the doors.

Because our clients wanted a traditional style, we took our design cues from the vernacular, taking the properties of an Irish farmhouse and giving it a contemporary twist. The beauty of these farmhouses is that they are horizontal buildings with low roofs, whereas dormer bungalows have high roofs. And the vernacular style is typically

Dermot Bannon Architects

one ... s in from two
... depth offers a
... e-plan dormer
... with a
... g has a
... r in the

We ... the
exist... to
run up ... a
has bee... garden, wit...

We introduce... ould
in the house, lik... zed wall and
breaking up surfa... vertical windows. But we
also celebrated solid parts, so we either had a lot
of glass or a lot of wall.

So while it is a very contemporary building and its
forms are designed in a modern way, the house
takes its cues from the vernacular.

PALETTE

Just as the house sits into the landscape, the
simple palette reflects it in black, greys and white.

The white render harks back to tradition. This
meets the black slate roof, which is in keeping with
the vernacular. We created a clean profile here
without overhangs, fascias, soffits or eaves.

We then used either grey materials or those that
would weather to grey in order to pick up on all the
greys in the landscape. The bay windows and flat-
roof sections are clad in zinc and the cladding is in
timber, which will naturally turn to grey over time.

Thus, the house becomes an integral part of the
landscape while the inhabitants can enjoy the
countryside around them, both from inside and
outside their home.

EPILOGUE

If you only take one thing from this book, I hope it is that good design has a fundamental impact on the quality of our lives. A house is not just about the structure and the materials – it's about how it makes you feel. Architecture and design are for everyone. Whether you are designing a house, an extension or just refitting your kitchen, there are so many opportunities to create something that has more meaning and function and brings a little joy and happiness into your life.

We should want and expect more from our homes. We should push for buildings that are designed for our individual needs and that also belong to the unique sites on which we build them.

It all starts with the brief and designing a home around the functions that you and your family need to live your individual lives. Houses are machines for living, and breaking away from the template houses we have become so used to and getting them to work and flow for you is the first step. Form follows function, so we need to start building from the inside out rather than the other way around.

Light is the key. Nothing lifts your spirits more than a house filled with natural light. Being aware of the light around your home and grabbing any opportunity you can to bring it in is probably the most fundamental way you can change how your house feels. Light is an amazing thing, and it's free!

I hope this book has shown that expanding your home is not just about extra floor space, but also about reaching out and enveloping the world around you, whether it's rolling countryside or a small city courtyard creating a connection to your individual part of the planet. Every site and home has unique opportunities in the form of vistas and views – capture them and make them part of your everyday life.

Each room in your house, from the kitchen to the bathroom to the bedroom, deserves to be the best it can be. No matter how big or small the space, there are techniques, materials and furnishings you can use that will change the room's atmosphere and create a better space. I hope this book has provided plenty of inspiration and knowledge of some of the possibilities available. We all aspire to and dream of a fantastic home, and I think everyone deserves a great space to live in. Not big, not grand, but light, bright and designed around *you*. A home to love.